The Right Blend

by Jennifer McClelland

Be Deliciously Healthy®

THE RIGHT BLEND

Blender-only

Raw Food Recipes

by Jennifer McClelland

Front cover photo of Jennifer: Tim Fischer
(www.fischer-photo.com)
Jennifer making nut milk photo: Tim Fischer
Cuisine photos: Jennifer McClelland
(www.bedeliciouslyhealthy.com)
Back cover photo/photos of Jennifer: Kirk Redlin
(www.redlinphoto.com)
Green smoothie photo: Geoff McClelland
(www.grasshopppercinema.com)
Dancing photos of Jennifer: Brady Eng

Published by
Be Deliciously Healthy®
Fruitland, ID 83619

Be Deliciously Healthy is a registered trademark of Jennifer McClelland and is used under license.

Library of Congress Cataloguing-in-Publication Data

McClelland, Jennifer
The Right Blend / Jennifer McClelland – 1st ed.

ISBN-13: 978-0615800738
ISBN-10: 0615800734
Library of Congress Control Number: 2013907869
CreateSpace Independent Publishing Platform
North Charleston, South Carolina

Disclaimer

The material in this book is for your information only and may not be construed as medical advice. The content provided is not intended to diagnose, cure, or treat any disease or ailment. Changing one's lifestyle for the better can produce cleansing reactions, and readers are advised to educate themselves and seek advice from a qualified health specialist when needed. Neither the author nor Be Deliciously Healthy® accepts liability or responsibility for any adverse consequences that one may experience during a lifestyle change.

DEDICATION

To Dad and Mom, thanks for your encouragement, support, and for being awesome parents!

Acknowledgements – MANY THANKS

To **Kristen Lum:** thank you for viewing my very first draft and encouraging me to keep recipes simple. To **Ms. Zhang Zhe:** your reminders that beauty must be coupled with the foods we eat were valued. To **Karen Yap, Lizzie Kukla,** and **Rachel Ward:** thank you, dear friends, for your edits and feedback. To **Stephanie Tebow:** thank you for your friendship and mentorship. Your wisdom came at the right time and in the right way. To **Susan Kleinschmidt:** thank you for your encouragement and accountability over the past few years. Coaching is a master art and you show that the true essence of a coach is one who believes in people and their future potential. To **Tim Fischer, Geoff McClelland,** and **Krista McClelland:** thank you for showing me food photography and food styling as well as trying out my healthy creations. I also thank **Cherie Soria**, **Dan Ladermann**, and the family at Living Light Culinary Institute, including **Kari Bernardi, Jenny Cornbleet, Matt Samuelson, Martine Lussier, Vinnette Thompson,** and **Drs. Rick** and **Karin Coleman Dina.**

TABLE of CONTENTS

Introduction

How can fresh fruits and vegetables transform a life? I entered my late teens feeling fatigued, bloated and clouded in my thinking. For over ten years, I suffered from Hashimoto's Thyroiditis, a form of hypothyroidism—otherwise known as an underactive thyroid—caused by an autoimmune deficiency. I'll never forget when the doctor said diseases are degenerative and my medication would increase with age. This was my fate, or so I thought.

Athletic since youth, it was hard to view myself as ill. I had a lot going for me. Growing up on a farm in Idaho, fresh air, clean water, and seasonal produce surrounded me. This was part of the benefits package that came with country living. I grew up in a small town called Fruitland. With a name like that, no wonder the peaches were sweeter, the plums juicier, and the apples crispier than any from supermarkets.

However, my idea of eating fresh fruits and vegetables was just something to *add* to processed meals as a healthy addition. A bowl of fruit or a green salad often accompanied larger portions of meat, dairy, and bread. I considered myself a healthy eater, preferring bottled juice over soda pop and whole wheat bread instead of bleached, white bread. However, the truth is I ate many over processed and additive-filled foods from cans, packages, and boxes labeled "healthier", "low fat", or "low calorie". Despite my efforts, my diet resembled too closely the Standard American Diet, also known as the S.A.D. diet. Little did I know killing the nutrients almost killed me.

This S.A.D. situation did not leave me hopeless. An optimist who needed answers, I wasn't about to give up. I once ran a marathon and decided walking wasn't an option. Unfortunately, I got lost after mile marker 24 by following a group of runners down the wrong trail. Confused and disappointed, I turned around and kept running—a feeble hobble resembling running—until I eventually reached the finish line. With this same spirit of determination, I combed through materials and books seeking ways to improve my health. Over the first few years I transitioned to eating more whole foods, such as cooked vegetables and grains. My health improved. However, it wasn't until I transitioned to eating a diet high in raw fruits, vegetables, nuts, and seeds that my symptoms disappeared.

Today I'm medication free. Now in my 30's, I have more energy and stamina than I did a decade ago. Do I believe eating raw food to be the cure for all ailments? No. But I'm convinced that my eating raw food played a critical role in my recovery. Eating raw provides the highest amount of vitamins, micronutrients, phytonutrients, and enzymes possible. I'm not one-hundred percent raw or strictly vegan, where no animal or honey bee products are eaten, but I eat a diet high in raw, plant-based foods. It's simple, eating raw gives you the most bang for your bite.

When I do cook foods I keep the ingredients as natural as possible, avoiding genetically modified foods (GMO – genetically modified organisms) and gluten. However, I find the "do not eat list" long, restrictive, and no fun. Instead, I enjoy turning vibrant and living fruits, vegetables, nuts, and seeds into delicious juices, smoothies, salads, sides, entrées, and desserts.

While many adhere to the raw food lifestyle to control serious health issues, some need a bit more motivation. As if preventing cancer and heart disease are not enough incentive to eat better, I share beauty tips with each recipe to provide inspiration to reach one's beauty potential naturally. My culinary lifestyle is where beauty and taste meet health and longevity. This is what I call a win-win situation!

Why Only a Blender?

As an American chef and instructor living and working between China and the U.S., I've used all types of kitchen appliances. From food processors to food dehydrators to ice cream makers, the tools and equipment used to make raw food cuisine are amazing. However, the electrical appliance I use the most is, hands down, a blender for its ease and convenience.

When I started teaching raw food classes in China, I noticed students were eager to try my dehydrated, or *unbaked*, granola and scones, but they were not willing to invest in the kitchen equipment necessary, such as a food dehydrator or food processor, to make my recipes.

Due to the cost, difficulty in sourcing, or the time-factor involved with many raw recipes, I centered most of my class recipes around a household blender. A commercial, high-speed blender and other electrical kitchen appliances I use at home or in private sessions with clients. Creating a full range of recipes using no more than a blender, a few kitchen tools, and recognizable ingredients for classes inspired me to write this book! Some of my recipes don't require a blender at all. A cutting board, knife, and bowl will do.

Blenders are easy to clean. They are also versatile. They blend smoothies, purée soups, crush ice, and grind nuts and seeds. I even use a blender to make cucumber and watermelon juice through blending and straining. Fresh juices are wonderful body quenchers and skin hydrators. If you have a juice machine, by all means use it. However, you don't need one for the juice recipes in this book.

Blenders normally hold 5 cups. Travel-size blenders also work, but the recipes in this book will need to be divided in half or in proportion to the size of the mini blender used. Lastly, you might be wondering what type of blender to use. There is a full range of blenders from conventional, household blenders to more expensive commercial, high-speed blenders. Most restaurants and smoothie bars use high-speed blenders. While I prefer a high-speed blender over a conventional blender, the recipes in this book accommodate both types. My suggestion is to start with the blender you have. If contemplating taking out a small loan to buy a commercial blender, start with the blender you have and work your way up. Remember, the best blender to have is the one you'll start using today!

Eating Raw for Beauty

As I transitioned to eating raw, the changes in my physical appearance were an added bonus to my newfound health. My face became clearer and less puffy. My dandruff-like skin turned supple and smooth. My hair, so fine and limp since I remember, began to grow fuller and stronger. In general, I experienced less bloating and inflammation throughout my entire body. I was sold. There was no turning back.

Start talking about achieving beautiful kidneys, a gorgeous liver, or an attractive colon through detoxification and living foods, and you may get deadpan stares or rolled eyes. Don't be discouraged. There are many who earnestly care about their health and take great strides to improve their eating habits. However, for those needing more incentive, share your natural beauty secrets for silky hair and luminous skin through the healing powers of raw food and a crowd of attentive listeners may soon gather. I share many of my natural beauty tips at www.dirtcheapbeautysecrets.com.

Raw foods nourish and beautify the outside because they are the best foods for the inside. Applying almond scrub to exfoliate the face or cucumbers to reduce puffy eyes seems like a perfectly normal thing to do. Is it strange to think eating raw almonds or fresh cucumbers will have a similar effect? In contrast, applying a barbecued pork chop as a facial mask is unimaginable and will most likely produce clogged pores and breakouts. Why expect a different result by placing it between two pieces of bread and eating it?

I once moved into an apartment with kitchen walls coated in cooked oils. It took hours of scrubbing the compacted, rancid oils before a glossy white appeared. Just as these cooked oils stuck to the stovetop and frying pans, not easily removed with running water or a gentle wipe, so do these toxins build up on the inside, clogging arteries, increasing blood pressure, and causing weight gain. If that's not bad news enough, speeding up the aging process and producing wrinkles.

In contrast to oils that undergo extreme temperatures of heat, natural oils and fats found in raw foods, on the other hand, nourish the skin and promote beauty as well as build internal health. Some of my favorite natural fats are found in avocados, coconuts, and cashews.

Raw foods also help maintain healthy skin through good hydration. I hydrate best with living water from fresh fruits and vegetables—juiced, blended, and eaten whole. Most mornings I start the day off with a fruit and vegetable juice, a green smoothie, or coconut water.

No More Excuses

Food is one of life's greatest pleasures, but too often the gastronomic bliss we feel from the comfort foods we love is short-lived until indigestion, heartburn, and bloating force us to ask, "Why did I eat that?" Beware of the potential pitfalls along the path to healthy eating and vibrant living. Roadblocks may come in the form of discouragement from others hindering you from making the lifestyle change to eating raw. They simply may not understand the health benefits of a raw diet, or they may fear the idea of eating fast food alone.

People often say we must splurge once in a while and everything must be done in moderation. Don't be fooled by this "group-speak". This advice sounds good because there is an element of truth in it. Finding balance in life is good, but the reality is people utter justifications for eating poorly because they simply have no better options available. Personally, I find it hard to limit myself to just *one* processed cookie or a *single* fried chip. How about a delicious balance of fruits, vegetables, nuts, and seeds, eaten as whole foods or in mouthwatering recipes? Imagine satiating the palate with delicious foods that nourish the body. Here are solutions for common excuses.

I'm too busy to cook. My recipes require a lot of blending, some chopping, and not a whole lot more. Busy people can bring a blender to work. Some actually travel with their blenders. A blended smoothie or soup takes no more than ten minutes to make—this includes washing the blender. For those with zero time for meal prep, eating whole foods is the way to go.

Eating healthy is too expensive. Good health is not reserved for the rich. Eating well does not mean buying imported products and expensive kitchen equipment. Buying local fruits and vegetables is often less expensive than packaged and ready-made meals. Although organic produce is typically more costly than conventional produce, for those who see a link between food and health, spending a little more upfront on quality saves more on medical bills down the road. In short, one cannot afford to eat poorly.

It's difficult to eat well when traveling. Road trips and overseas excursions are wonderful opportunities to experience new flavors and textures. However, traveling can break a normal routine. While packing favorite foods and supplements help, it may not sustain the entire trip. Upon arrival, locate the nearest grocery store or local wet market. Larger international supermarkets tend to have organic sections.

I like my junk food. Bad habits are hard to break. While one does not have to be militant about eating perfect, discovering flavors in natural ingredients and actually craving raw foods is much easier once the body is cleansed, which I discuss in the back of this book. Start with my recipes and begin to make a list of healthy alternatives to replace junk food cravings. For instance, an apple or trail mix on hand helps prevent eating junk food on impulse.

I can't eat healthy and be social. Food choices must not alienate one from friends and meeting new people. While most restaurants offer something healthy on the menu, options are often limited. I remind myself that fellowship is more important than my food selection, and I often drink a smoothie or put trail mix and an apple in my purse before going out. Try hosting healthy dinners and sharing recipes with friends. Lastly, lecturing friends on their poor food choices (especially while they are eating) is a turn off. A little tact goes a long way and your most convincing argument will be your own glorious transformation.

JENNIFER'S RAW BASICS

Jennifer's Shopping List

This shopping list provides the food and kitchen tools needed for the recipes in this book. Your range of produce will vary depending on your geographical location and seasonal selection. For this reason, I don't often list specific types and varieties of produce, such as *Shiitake* mushrooms, *Roma* tomatoes, or *Granny Smith* apples. When I do specify a certain produce, feel free to exchange it for the type available at your local market. The transition and sustainability of your eating more living foods depend on the simplicity and ease in making the recipes as well as sourcing affordable and accessible produce. Hence, use this list as a guideline.

Produce marked with an asterisk (*) is stored on the countertop. When countertop produce reaches its ripeness, it's time to eat them or move them to the refrigerator to slow down the ripening process. Nuts and seeds can be refrigerated, but if the weather is cool they can be stored in the pantry. Cold-pressed oils are heat-sensitive and storing them in the refrigerator gives them a longer shelf life. If oils smell rancid discard them.

Coconut oil is an exception and can be stored in the pantry due to its stability in cool temperatures. Coconut oil is often solid and liquefies around 75˚F/24˚C. If the weather is warm, move the coconut oil to the refrigerator. When my recipes call for coconut oil, this means in liquefied form. To liquefy, add the amount needed to a bowl and place the bowl inside a larger bowl of hot water for a few minutes.

Produce

Apples
Avocados*
Bananas*
Beet Root
Bell Peppers*
Blueberries
Broccoli
Cabbage
Cantaloupe
Carrots

Cauliflower
Celery
Cherries
Cherry Tomatoes
Coconuts*
Corn (sweet)
Cucumbers
Ginger
Honeydew
Lemons*

Limes*
Mangos*
Mushrooms
Onions*
Oranges*
Pears
Raspberries
Sprouts
(alfalfa, broccoli, soybean, etc.)

Strawberries
Tomatoes

Watermelon*
Zucchini

Leafy Greens and Herbs

Basil
Cilantro
Collard Greens
Dill

Green Onions
Kale
Parsley
Peppermint

Romaine Lettuce
Spinach

Spices

Black Pepper
Cayenne
Chili

Cinnamon
Curry Powder
Garlic Powder

Nutmeg
Onion Powder
White Pepper

Dried Fruits, Nuts, & Seeds

Almonds
Cashews
Coconut Flour or Shreds
Dates (honey, medjool,
and red/jujube)
Flax Seeds

Macadamia Nuts
Pecans
Pistachios
Pumpkin Seeds
Raisins

Sesame Seeds
(black and white)
Sundried Tomatoes
Sunflower Seeds
Walnuts

Cold-pressed Oils

Coconut Oil
Flax Seed Oil

Olive Oil
Sesame Oil

Sweeteners

Agave Nectar

Maple Syrup

Raw Honey

Other

Apple Cider Vinegar
Liquid Aminos
(natural soy sauce)
Cacao Powder
Carob Powder
Chlorella Powder
Grass Powders

(barley and wheat)
Maca Powder
Miso
Nori Seaweed Sheets
Nutritional Yeast
Peppermint Oil Extract
Sea Salt

Spirulina Powder
Vanilla Extract

Kitchen Tools

8- or 10-inch Chef's Knife
9-inch Pie Plate
9-inch Spring Form Pan
9-inch Tart Pan
Bamboo Sushi Mat
Grater
Kitchen Scissors
Lemon Press or
Handheld Juicer
Measuring Cups
and Spoons
Melon Ball Scooper
(optional)
Mixing Bowls
Nut Milk Bag
or Cheesecloth
Paper Towels
Paring Knife
Parchment Paper
Peeler
Rubber Spatula
Serrated Knife
Spiral Slicer (optional)
Strainer
Toothpicks
Wooden Cutting Board

Glossary for Special Ingredients

Apple Cider Vinegar adds a zing to many salads, dressings, and sauces. Look for brands that are organic, unfiltered, unheated, and unpasteurized.

Cacao Powder is derived from the cacao bean. It's chocolate in its purest form. Cacao powder comes in toasted and raw forms. Raw cacao is hailed as a superfood for its rich mineral content and abundance in antioxidants. However, cacao can act as a stimulant, and some use it sparingly or substitute it with carob powder.

Carob Powder is a mineral-rich substance from the carob pod, which is derived from the carob tree. Carob is sweeter and less bitter than cacao. Although carob has a distinctly different flavor than cacao, they are often used interchangeably in recipes. Carob powder also comes in toasted and raw forms.

Chlorella is green algae known for its nutrient density. In addition to being rich in vitamins, minerals, amino acids (proteins), and chlorophyll, chlorella aids in ridding the body of toxins and heavy metals.

Liquid Aminos is a natural soy sauce. This gluten-free liquid protein concentrate is great in soups, dressings, and dips. Look for organic and non-GMO brands.

Maca is a Peruvian root known for enhancing stamina and energy. Traditionally used to increase fertility in women and boost libido in men, maca powder adds a wonderful malty flavor and creaminess to milkshakes and desserts.

Miso is a fermented soybean paste used in many Asian cuisines for its depth of flavor and saltiness. A favorite type of miso is Japanese light-colored miso. Look for organic and non-GMO brands.

Nutritional Yeast comes in powder or flakes and is commonly mistaken for brewer's yeast. Despite its unappealing name, nutritional yeast boasts a nutty, cheesy flavor. It is known for its amino acids (proteins) and B-complex vitamins.

Sea Salt is natural salt, often colored with pink and grey tones. Sea salt is not to be mistaken for common table salt, which is stripped of trace minerals through a chemical bleaching process. To cut back on salt in general, natural sodium is obtained through eating sodium-rich foods, such as celery, coconut water, and sea vegetables.

Spirulina is a blue-green algae and boasts a high source of calcium and protein. Like chlorella, this algae contains rich sources of vitamins, minerals, and chlorophyll. It also cleanses the body of toxins and heavy metals.

Sweeteners used in my recipes include dried fruits, raw honey, maple syrup, and agave nectar. Raw honey is unrefined and unprocessed. It's known for its anti-bacterial, anti-viral, and enzymatic properties. Depending on one's dietary needs and personal preferences, honey can be interchanged with agave nectar, a sweet golden syrup derived from the agave plant. Maple syrup is an amber-colored liquid derived from the sap of maple trees and carries a deep, woody flavor. Maple syrup, and sometimes agave nectar, is not considered raw as heat is used in the extraction process.

More Helpful Tips

On Washing Produce
Soak produce for 10 to 15 minutes in a bowl of water with a few spoonfuls of apple cider vinegar, an anti-bacterial disinfectant, and then rinse. There are several products to wash produce with. Use brands containing chemical-free and natural ingredients.

On Organic
The best food to eat is organic food grown at home. For compost and gardening tips visit **www.hamanishifarms.com**. The next best thing is to buy locally grown organic produce. The first two options are not always possible so look for foods with organic labels in stores. Keep in mind that eating organic does not have to be an all-or-nothing approach. It's especially difficult when traveling or eating at restaurants so do the best you can.

On Cutting Boards
Choose wooden cutting boards over plastic. Not only are there natural properties to fight bacteria in wooden cutting boards, they do not dull knives like plastic cutting boards do. Any type of cross-contamination must be avoided. Since the following recipes call for fruits, vegetables, nuts, and seeds, there is no cross-contamination with animal products.

Basics in Nut and Seed Milks

Nut and seed milks are creamy and nutritious beverages. Used in smoothies, sauces, soups, and desserts, these creamy liquids are perfect for anyone desiring a nutritional boost or searching for a non-dairy replacement. Keep a stash of your favorite nuts and seeds in the pantry to make these milks in no time.

Most of the time, nut and seed milks are drank the same day they are made, but they can be stored in the refrigerator up to two days. When stored, give them a good shake or swirl in the blender before drinking. In addition, these milks can be frozen in ice cube trays and then transferred to an airtight container for later use in smoothies and milkshakes. I provide some favorite nut and seed milk recipes in this book, but the following guidelines allow you to create your own so you don't rely on recipes alone.

Step 1 – Soaking

Directions: Soak nuts or seeds in water, drain, and rinse.

Soaking starts the germination process, releasing tannins and neutralizing enzyme inhibitors. Soaking not only allows the body to better absorb nutrients, it also tones down any bitterness in the nut or seed. The soaking time depends on size. For example, almonds need 8 hours soaking time while sunflower seeds need 2 hours. Discard the acidic and tinted soaking water. I admit I'm not one to use a chart or timer. I often soak my nuts and seeds overnight, no matter the size, in a cool place or in the refrigerator. There are also times when I forget to soak my nuts or seeds, and I'll soak them for just a few minutes before using. If they soak longer then the allotted time, drain, rinse, and replace the soaking water with fresh water at least once a day and up to two days in the refrigerator.

Step 2 – Blending

Directions: Blend the nuts or seeds with pure water to form a thick mixture.

The ratio of nuts and seeds to water depends on the creaminess and thickness desired. For the milk recipes I provide in this book there are two different consistencies: regular and cream. For regular, use one part nuts or seeds to three, or more, parts water. For cream, use one part nuts or seeds to two parts, or less, water. Blend in a favorite sweetener, such as a spoonful of honey, agave nectar, or maple syrup. A few drops of stevia or a couple pitted dates are also good choices.

Step 3 – Straining

Directions: Pour the liquid mixture into a bowl lined with a nut milk bag or cheesecloth. With one hand holding the top of the bag, use the other hand to gently squeeze from the bottom, allowing the liquid to fill the bowl.

When I first started making nut and seed milks I used a clean, white t-shirt as a mesh strainer. Living overseas, this invention was birthed out of necessity. A Chinese mesh cloth, used for steaming buns in bamboo baskets or making tofu works similar to cheesecloth. For some creams, such as cashew cream, the straining process is omitted.

Step 4 – Saving Pulp

Directions: Store the leftover nut and seed pulp in a sealed bag or airtight container in the freezer up to 2 months. Thaw the pulp a few hours before using.

Nothing needs to be wasted. The nutritious, leftover pulp can be used as flour in dehydrated, or even traditional, crusts, cookies, and breads. In addition, this pulp also makes a natural exfoliator and is used in my *Nourishing Facial & Body Polish* recipe in the section, *Lifestyle Tips and Beauty Recipes*

On Coconut Milk

Coconut milk, not to be confused with coconut water, is made from the white meat blended with water to form a milk or cream. I prefer to blend coconut meat with pure water, instead of coconut water, because it does not separate as easy. The best types of coconuts to make milk are young coconuts, often from Southeast Asia, called young Thai coconuts. The meat is a soft, jelly and, like cashews, does not need straining. However, young coconuts may be difficult to source. I recommend a simplified version of coconut milk by using fresh shelled coconut or dried coconut flakes and following the steps I provide for nut and seed milks. This method will need straining and the leftover pulp can be stored in the freezer in an airtight container and used as coconut flour.

Get the Green Smoothie Edge

WARNING! Green smoothies may contain fresh, organic leafy green vegetables and fruits, which are loaded with nutrients needed for healthy hair, skin, and nails. If signs of improved digestion, mental clarity, and increased energy levels result, contact your local farmer for a consultation on the full range of organic produce available. In the case of weight loss or an improved appearance, contact a style consultant immediately for a new wardrobe and makeover. Make a green smoothie now before this offer expires—or you do!

How can a green colored drink produce die-hard, green smoothie converts? Popularized by Victoria Boutenko, green smoothies are a combination of leafy greens sweetened with fruits. It's a liquid, power-packed meal. I was in a bit of shock when I encountered my first group of green smoothie drinkers. At the breakfast bar, I quickly poured myself a green smoothie to fit in. It was hard not to notice how amazing some of these people looked. Some appeared 10 to 15 years younger than their age. Even those over 60 years old had a glow others their age lacked. They seemed confident, almost arrogant, carrying around glass jars of green concoctions consisting of blended leafy greens and fruits. Most of these people ate a raw plant-based diet, and green smoothies seemed to be the star player in their morning regimen.

This green smoothie encounter took me back to when I was growing up in the country. Cows and horses grazed on green grasses in fields all day long. At times they ate dried alfalfa, grains, or licked a mineral salt block. However, much of their diet consisted of fresh vegetation. With coats of hair so luminous and shiny and physical builds so muscular and lean, I contemplated why humans didn't compare in such beauty and strength. What if I ate the same way and switched to eating grass all day? Unfortunately, I dismissed the notion of chewing weeds as nonsense.

Years later, I was confronted with people in their 40's, 50's, and 60's who were in excellent health and ate a diet similar to the animals I saw in the fields. What better way to get all this goodness packed into one meal than by drinking a green smoothie? Fruits add a healthy load of carbohydrates, fiber, antioxidants, and nutrients. Likewise, leafy greens are like superior multi-vitamins with minerals and phytonutrients packed into every leaf. The chlorophyll gives leaves their vibrant shades of green through the absorption of sunlight, working as internal healers and cleansers.

Although I love leafy greens in salads, I found that in order to increase the amount of greens in my diet, a blended green smoothie or green juice increased my nutrient intake as well as improved my digestion. Whether for breakfast, a meal, or a snack drinking a green smoothie is like sipping the sun's pure energy.

Building Blocks for Making Green Smoothies

Green smoothies are often a 60 to 40 percent ratio of fruits to leafy greens. They can also be a 50 to 50 ratio of fruits and veggies. Yet, another type of green smoothie is one with almost all greens and half an orange or squeeze of lemon to cut the bitterness of the greens. It must be obvious by now that there are no strict rules for making green smoothies. Nevertheless, there are some guidelines to follow. I provide green smoothie recipes in this book, but put aside your measuring cups and spoons for now and learn how to make them on your own.

Step One – Choose Leafy Greens

Choose one, two, or three leafy greens such as romaine lettuce, kale, and spinach. I tend to choose leafy greens without too much pungency so they don't overpower the fruitiness of the smoothie. Alternating the variety of greens offers a broader spectrum of nutrients.

Step Two – Choose Fruits

Choose one, two, or three fruits such as oranges, lemons, limes, bananas, mangos, pineapples, blueberries, and raspberries. Think of another fruit? Great! But do avoid melons in smoothies as they digest better eaten alone. Changing fruits from day to day offers a wider range of nutrients.

Step Three – Add Supplements

This step is optional. In small amounts, add some pungent herbs such as parsley, mint, basil, or cilantro. You can also add powders such as chlorella, spirulina, young wheat grass, and young barley grass. Supplements are good boosters and are great to bring on trips when eating enough greens is a challenge.

Step Four – Blend

Add some water or juice to the leafy greens and blend until smooth. Then add the fruits. Most drink green smoothies at room temperature for optimum digestion, but ice cubes can be added. Add any frozen fruit chunks or ice cubes in gradually.

DRINKS

Basil-Infused Cucumber Juice

Cucumbers are wonderful skin cleansers as well as bloating and swelling preventers. The leftover pulp is used in my *Radiating Cucumber Mask* in the section, *Lifestyle Tips and Beauty Recipes.*

5 cups thinly sliced cucumbers   **2 tablespoons lemon juice**
1/2 cup water   **1 tablespoon minced basil leaves**
2 tablespoons honey or agave nectar   **1/2 teaspoon spirulina or chlorella**

Blend all ingredients together until smooth. If using a high-speed blender, the cucumbers can be coarsely chopped. Strain through a nut milk bag or cheesecloth. Drink immediately. **SERVES 2**

Watermelon Juice with a Hint of Peppermint

Watermelon and mint are excellent detoxifiers and skin cleansers. Mint is known for its therapeutic qualities, improving mood and circulation.

5 cups finely chopped watermelon   **1 pinch sea salt**
3 tablespoons minced peppermint leaves

Blend all ingredients together. If using a high-speed blender, the watermelon can be coarsely chopped. Strain through a nut milk bag or cheesecloth if desired. Drink immediately. **SERVES 2**

Basil-Infused Cucumber Juice

Lemon Ginger Detox

This drink hydrates, detoxifies, and improves circulation.

4 cups warm water
1/4 cup lemon juice
1 tablespoon grated ginger

2 tablespoons honey
1/4 teaspoon cinnamon

Blend or stir the ingredients together. Use hot water if desired. **SERVES 2**

Coconut Water Skin Cleanser

Coconut water hydrates skin back to its youthful suppleness.

3 cups coconut water
(or water from one coconut)

1 tablespoon minced peppermint leaves

Blend all ingredients together. Strain through a nut milk bag or cheesecloth if desired. Drink immediately. **SERVES 2**

Ruby Red Blush

This sweet red elixir is like blush for the skin and helps reduce puffiness and dark circles under the eye area.

2 cups thinly sliced cucumbers
1 cup thinly sliced celery
1/2 cup water

1/2 cup finely diced beet root
(beet leaves optional)
1/4 cup chopped parsley

Blend all ingredients together. If using a high-speed blender, the cucumbers, celery, beet root, and parley can be coarsely chopped. Strain through a nut milk bag or cheesecloth. Drink immediately. **SERVES 2**

Ruby Red Blush

Almond Milk

Almonds provide an excellent source of protein and calcium. They are also rich in vitamin E, which aids in the prevention of facial lines and wrinkles. The leftover pulp can be used in my *Nourishing Facial & Body Polish* in the section, *Lifestyle Tips and Beauty Recipes*.

1 cup almonds, soaked 8 hours, drained, and rinsed
3 cups water

2 tablespoons honey or agave nectar
1 teaspoon vanilla extract
1 pinch sea salt

Blend all ingredients together until smooth. Strain through a nut milk bag or cheesecloth. Drink immediately or refrigerate in an airtight container up to 2 days.
SERVES 2

Pumpkin Seed Milk

The natural, raw oils in pumpkin seeds help keep skin radiant. The leftover pulp can be used in my *Nourishing Facial & Body Polish* in the section, *Lifestyle Tips and Beauty Recipes*.

1 cup pumpkin seeds, soaked 4 to 6 hours, drained, and rinsed
3 cups water

2 tablespoons honey or agave nectar
1 teaspoon vanilla extract
1 pinch sea salt

Blend all ingredients together until smooth. Strain through a nut milk bag or cheesecloth. Drink immediately or refrigerate in an airtight container up to 2 days.
SERVES 2

Almond Milk

Sesame Seed Milk

Sesame seeds are a beauty aid for skin cell renewal and hair health. The leftover pulp can be used in my *Nourishing Facial & Body Polish* in the section, *Lifestyle Tips and Beauty Recipes*.

1 cup white sesame seeds*, soaked 2 hours, drained, and rinsed
3 cups water
1 pinch sea salt

1/2 cup dates (honey or medjool), pitted and packed
1 tablespoon maple syrup
2 teaspoons vanilla extract

Blend all ingredients together until smooth. Strain through a nut milk bag or cheesecloth. Drink immediately or refrigerate in an airtight container up to 2 days.
SERVES 2

*White sesame seeds can be replaced with black sesame seeds.

Black Beauty

Black sesame seeds strengthen the liver and kidneys, which support hair health. These seeds have been traditionally used to prevent premature graying of hair.

3/4 cup almonds, soaked 8 hours, drained, and rinsed
3/4 cup red (jujube) dates, pitted and packed

1/2 cup black sesame seeds, soaked 2 hours, drained, and rinsed
3 cups water
1 pinch sea salt

Blend all ingredients together until smooth. Strain through a nut milk bag or cheesecloth.Drink immediately or refrigerate in an airtight container up to 2 days.
SERVES 2

Black Beauty

Sweet Almond and Red Date Cream

Red dates are known in China for their anti-aging and blood nourishing properties. This cream can be poured over a bowl of fresh berries or added to a favorite tea. The leftover pulp can be used in my *Nourishing Facial & Body Polish* in the section, *Lifestyle Tips and Beauty Recipes*.

1 cup almonds, soaked 8 hours, drained, and rinsed
1 cup red (jujubes) dates*, pitted and packed

2 cups water
1 teaspoon vanilla extract
1 pinch sea salt

Blend all ingredients together until smooth. Strain through a nut milk bag or cheesecloth. Use immediately or refrigerate in an airtight container up to 2 days.
MAKES OVER 3 CUPS

*Red (jujube) dates can be replaced with honey or medjool dates.

SMOOTHIES

Spinach, Mango, and Banana Smoothie

Fresh spinach is a rich source of vitamin A, aiding in the elimination of acne and skin problems.

2 cups spinach, packed
2 bananas
2 medium mangos
1 cup water

1/4 cup lemon juice
1/2 teaspoon spirulina or chlorella
2 cups ice cubes (optional)

Blend all ingredients together until smooth, pulsing in the ice cubes gradually. Drink immediately. **SERVES 2**

Peppermint Cacao Energy Surge

The raw oil in pumpkin seeds helps keep the skin soft and elastic.

2 cups *Pumpkin Seed Milk*
(see recipe page 26)
2 bananas, fresh or frozen slices
2 tablespoons cacao or carob powder
2 tablespoons honey or agave nectar
1 tablespoon maca powder

1/2 teaspoon spirulina or chlorella
10 peppermint leaves or 1 drop
peppermint oil extract
1 pinch sea salt
2 cups ice cubes (optional)

Blend all ingredients together until smooth, pulsing in the frozen ingredients gradually. To add the peppermint oil extract, dip a clean toothpick in the oil and add one drop from the toothpick. For a stronger mint flavor, repeat the step with a clean toothpick. Blend again. Drink immediately. **SERVES 2**

Nuts for a Choco-Banana Smoothie

Bananas are a rich source of potassium and vitamin C. They help reduce puffy eyes often caused by eating too much table salt (sodium chloride).

2 cups *Almond Milk* (see recipe page 26)
2 bananas, fresh or frozen slices
1/2 cup dates (honey or medjool), pitted and packed
1/4 cup cashews, soaked 2 hours, drained, and rinsed
2 tablespoons cacao or carob powder

2 tablespoons honey or agave nectar (optional)
1 tablespoon maca powder
1/4 teaspoon cinnamon
1 pinch sea salt
2 cups ice cubes (optional)

Blend all ingredients together until smooth, pulsing in the frozen ingredients gradually. Drink immediately. **SERVES 2**

Kale and Pineapple Smoothie

The super-rich nutrients and vitamins in kale aid in skin regeneration, which counter the effects of aging and skin damage.

2 cups chopped kale, packed
1 cup diced pineapple
1 banana

1 cup water
2 tablespoons lemon or lime juice
2 cups ice cubes (optional)

Blend all ingredients together until smooth, pulsing in the ice cubes gradually. Drink immediately. **SERVES 1**

Nuts for a Choco-Banana Smoothie

with *Jewelry for the Dinner Table*
by Jennifer

Cherry Celery Slush

Celery provides a source of natural sodium and prevents water retention. It also works as a natural laxative.

1 1/2 cups pitted cherries, fresh or frozen
1 cup chopped celery
1 cup diced pineapple, fresh or frozen

1/2 cup water
1-inch cube beet root
2 cups ice cubes

Blend all ingredients together until smooth, pulsing in the frozen ingredients gradually. Drink immediately. **SERVES 1 TO 2**

Raspberry Greenade

Young sprouts contain abundant amounts of enzymes, minerals, and chlorophyll, nourishing the blood for strong hair and firm skin.

2 cups alfalfa or broccoli sprouts, packed
2 cups raspberries, fresh or frozen
1 medium mango
1/2 cup water

2 tablespoons lemon juice
1 teaspoon young wheat or barley grass powder
2 cups ice cubes (optional)

Blend all the ingredients together until smooth, pulsing in the frozen ingredients gradually. Drink immediately. **SERVES 2**

Cherry Celery Slush

Mango Wake-Up Call

The leftover mango seed from this smoothie is a great exfoliator for the skin. Gently rub the face and neck with the mango seed before showering.

3 1/2 cups *Almond Milk*
(see recipe page 26)
1 cup sliced mangos, fresh or frozen
2 tablespoons honey or agave nectar

2 tablespoons maca powder
1/4 teaspoon cayenne
1 pinch sea salt
2 cups ice cubes (optional)

Blend all ingredients together until smooth, pulsing in the frozen ingredients gradually. Drink immediately. **SERVES 2**

Strawberry Calcium Boost

Strawberries are a rich source of silicon needed for strong hair, skin, and nails. Black sesame seeds provide a rich source of calcium.

2 1/2 cups strawberries
2 bananas
1 cup water

1/4 cup black sesame seeds, soaked 2
hours, drained, and rinsed
2 tablespoons honey or agave nectar

Blend all ingredients together until smooth. Drink immediately. **SERVES 2**

Mango Wake-Up Call

Citrus Cucumber Crush

Cucumber peel provides a rich source of silicon, improving hair, skin, and nail growth.

3 cups sliced cucumbers, frozen
1 cup orange juice
1/4 cup lemon juice
3 tablespoons honey or agave nectar

2 tablespoons lime juice
2 pinches sea salt
1 cup ice cubes

Use a lemon press or handheld juicer to make the citrus juices. Blend all ingredients together until smooth, pulsing in the frozen ingredients gradually. Drink immediately. **SERVES 2**

I "C" Smoothie

Blueberries keep skin firm and contain powerful antioxidants that protect the body from free radicals, which cause damage to collagen.

2 bananas, fresh or frozen slices
1 cup blueberries, fresh or frozen
1 medium mango
1 medium orange

1 cup water
2 teaspoons grated ginger
2 cups ice cubes (optional)

Blend all ingredients together until smooth, pulsing in the frozen ingredients gradually. Drink immediately. **SERVES 2**

Citrus Cucumber Crush

SOUPS

Curried Mango Bisque

Mango enzymes keep the face radiant and help prevent acne breakouts.

2 1/2 cups mango cubes or slices,
fresh or frozen
1 1/4 cups pumpkin seeds, soaked 4 to 6
hours, drained, and rinsed
1 1/4 cups water

1/2 cup orange juice
1/2 teaspoon curry powder
1 or 2 pinches cayenne
1 pinch sea salt (optional)

GARNISH
Cayenne

To make the pumpkin seed cream, blend the pumpkin seeds and the water together until smooth. Strain through a nut milk bag or cheesecloth. Use a lemon press or handheld juicer to make the orange juice. Blend the pumpkin seed cream, orange juice, mango, spices, and salt until smooth. Garnish each bowl with a pinch of cayenne. Serve immediately or refrigerate in an airtight container up to 2 days.
SERVES 4

Curried Mango Bisque

Cauliflower Soup

Cauliflower is a natural anti-inflammatory, keeping puffiness and bloating at bay.

3 cups chopped cauliflower
2 cups *Almond Milk* (see recipe page 26)
1/2 cup cashews, soaked 2 hours,
drained, and rinsed
1 teaspoon onion powder

2 tablespoons liquid aminos or
natural soy sauce
1/2 teaspoon black pepper
1/2 teaspoon garlic powder
1/2 teaspoon sea salt

GARNISHES
Minced parsley
Black pepper

Blend the cashews and almond milk until smooth. Add the remaining ingredients and blend again until smooth. Garnish each bowl of soup with a pinch of minced parsley and a dash of black pepper. Serve immediately or refrigerate in an airtight container up to 2 days. **SERVES 4 TO 6**

Creamy Broccoli Bisque

Broccoli is a true skin beautifier. The vitamin C, sulfur, and amino acids in broccoli remove toxins and keep rashes, boils, and tough-looking skin away.

3 cups chopped broccoli
2 cups water
3/4 cup cashews, soaked 2 hours,
drained, and rinsed
1/4 cup chopped onions

2 tablespoons miso
2 teaspoons onion powder
1 teaspoon garlic powder
1/4 teaspoon black pepper
1/4 teaspoon sea salt

GARNISH
Broccoli florets

Blend the cashews and water until smooth. Add the remaining ingredients and blend again. Garnish each bowl of bisque with 2 or 3 little broccoli florets. Serve immediately or refrigerate in an airtight container up to 2 days. **SERVES 4 TO 6**

Cream of Celery

Not only is celery known to reduce stress, it is also a natural tooth cleanser, dissolving stains on tooth enamel.

3 cups chopped celery
1 1/2 cups water
1/4 cup cashews, soaked 2 hours,
drained, and rinsed
1 tablespoon miso
1 tablespoon chopped parsley

1/2 teaspoon onion powder
1/4 teaspoon black pepper
1/4 teaspoon garlic powder
1/4 teaspoon minced garlic
1 pinch cayenne
1 pinch sea salt (optional)

GARNISHES
Cayenne
Black pepper

Blend the cashews and water until smooth. Add the remaining ingredients and blend again. Garnish each bowl of soup with a dash of cayenne and black pepper. Serve immediately or refrigerate in an airtight container up to 2 days. **SERVES 4**

Tomato Ginger Bisque

This silicon-rich bisque beautifies the hair, skin, and nails.

3 cups finely chopped tomatoes,
deseeded
1 cup finely chopped red bell peppers,
deseeded
1/4 cup cashews, soaked 2 hours,
drained, and rinsed
1/4 cup sundried tomatoes, soaked
1 hour and drained

2 tablespoons minced parsley
1 tablespoon olive oil
1 tablespoon miso
1 tablespoon grated ginger
1/2 teaspoon onion powder
1/4 teaspoon garlic powder
1/4 teaspoon white pepper
1/4 teaspoon sea salt

GARNISHES
1/4 cup *Onion Sour Cream* (see recipe page 64)
2 tablespoons finely diced green onions

Blend the peppers, tomatoes, sundried tomatoes, and cashews until smooth. Add the remaining ingredients and blend again. A little water may need to be added depending on the water content of the tomatoes. To garnish, top with *Onion Sour Cream* (see recipe page 64) and a few green onions. Serve immediately. **SERVES 4**

Tomato Ginger Bisque

with *Jewelry for the Dinner Table*
by Jennifer

Carrot Ginger Soup

Carrots contain a high level of beta-carotene, protecting against cell damage and the aging process.

3 cups chopped carrots
3/4 cup water
1/4 cup cashews, soaked 2 hours, drained, and rinsed
2 tablespoons grated ginger
1 tablespoon miso

1 tablespoon liquid aminos or natural soy sauce
1 tablespoon minced parsley
2 teaspoons onion powder
1/4 teaspoon white pepper

GARNISH
Sprigs of parsley

Blend the cashews and water until smooth. Add the remaining ingredients and blend again. Garnish each bowl of soup with a sprig of parsley. Serve immediately or refrigerate in an airtight container up to 2 days. **SERVES 4**

Yellow Bell Pepper Bisque with Basil

Bell pepper and tomato skins contain rich sources of silicon needed for strong hair, skin, and nails. Ripe bell peppers are hues of yellow and red.

2 cups finely chopped yellow bell peppers, deseeded
2 cups yellow cherry tomatoes
1/2 cup cashews, soaked 2 hours, drained, and rinsed
2 tablespoons minced basil

2 tablespoons miso
2 teaspoons olive oil
2 teaspoons flax seed oil
1/4 teaspoon black pepper
1/4 teaspoon onion powder
1 pinch sea salt

GARNISH
Basil leaves

Blend the peppers, tomatoes, cashews, and miso until smooth. Add the spices and salt and blend again. With the blender running, add the oils and then pulse in the minced basil. Garnish the bisque with whole basil leaves. Serve immediately. **SERVES 4 TO 6**

Carrot Ginger Soup

Summer Gazpacho

This gazpacho is loaded with vitamin C, illuminating the skin.

2 1/2 cups chopped tomatoes + 1 cup finely diced tomatoes
1/2 cup chopped cucumbers + 1/2 cup finely diced cucumbers
1/2 cup chopped red bell peppers + 1/2 cup finely diced red bell peppers
1/4 cup chopped onions
1 tablespoon apple cider vinegar

1/4 cup sundried tomatoes, soaked 1 hour in 1/2 cup water (do not drain)
2 tablespoons minced cilantro
1 tablespoon olive oil
1 tablespoon miso
1/2 teaspoon cayenne
1/4 teaspoon sea salt

GARNISHES
1 avocado, diced
1/2 cup *Onion Sour Cream* (see recipe page 64)
2 tablespoons minced cilantro

Blend the sundried tomatoes with the 1/2 cup soaking water until smooth. Add the chopped tomatoes, cucumbers, red bell peppers, and onions until smooth. Add the apple cider vinegar, miso, olive oil, cayenne, and salt and blend again. In a large bowl, pour the blended mixture in with the finely diced tomatoes, cucumbers, red bell peppers, and minced cilantro and stir. To garnish each bowl, add diced avocados, a dollop of *Onion Sour Cream*, and minced cilantro. Serve immediately or refrigerate in an airtight container up to 2 days. **SERVES 4 TO 6**

Summer Gazpacho

Creamy Apple Ginger Soup

The water soluble vitamins B and C in apples nourish the skin. Apples also help reduce dark circles under the eyes.

3 cups chopped apples
2 cups water
1/2 cup cashews, soaked 2 hours, drained, and rinsed
2 tablespoons lemon juice

1/2 cup dates (honey or medjool), pitted and packed
1 tablespoon grated ginger
1/4 teaspoon cinnamon
1 pinch sea salt (optional)

GARNISHES
1/4 cup finely diced apples
Cinnamon

Blend the apples, water, and ginger until smooth. Strain through a nut milk bag or cheesecloth. Pour the liquid back into the blender and add the remaining ingredients and blend until smooth. Garnish each bowl with a spoonful of finely diced apples and a pinch of cinnamon. Serve immediately or refrigerate in an airtight container up to 2 days. **SERVES 4**

Chilled Mango and Coconut Cream Soup

The fruit acids in mangos exfoliate the skin and promote skin cell renewal. This soup can be served as a light dessert as well.

2 1/2 cups mango cubes or slices, frozen
1 1/2 cups dried coconut meat or
coconut flakes
1 1/2 cups water

1 cup diced oranges, frozen
1/2 cup orange juice
2 tablespoons minced peppermint leaves
1 pinch sea salt

GARNISHES
1/4 cup coconut cream
Peppermint leaves

Blend the coconut meat and the water until smooth. Strain the blended mixture through a nut milk bag or cheesecloth. Set aside 1/4 cup coconut cream for garnishing and put the rest back in the blender. Use a lemon press or handheld juicer to make the orange juice. Blend the coconut cream, mango, orange juice, and salt until smooth. Pulse in the minced peppermint leaves. To garnish, drizzle coconut cream over the soup with a couple peppermint leaves. Serve immediately.
SERVES 4 to 6

SALADS AND DRESSINGS

Melon Ball Medley

Melons are full of living water, quenching and hydrating the skin.

4 cups cantaloupe melon balls
4 cups honeydew melon balls
3 tablespoons lemon juice

2 tablespoons minced peppermint leaves
1 or 2 pinches sea salt

Use a melon ball scooper to form melon balls. Another option is to cut the melons into cubes. In a large bowl, gently fold in the remaining ingredients. Serve immediately or refrigerate in an airtight container up to 2 days. **SERVES 6 TO 8**

Emergency Salad Dressing

In addition to calcium and iron, sesame seeds are a rich source of copper, a mineral needed in the formation of collagen for healthy skin.

2 tablespoons lemon juice
1 tablespoon olive oil or flax seed oil
1 tablespoon white sesame seeds

2 teaspoons honey or agave nectar
1 pinch sea salt

Add ingredients directly to a salad and toss. **SERVES 1 TO 2**

Melon Ball Medley

Creamy Cashew Dill Dressing

Cashews are a good source of zinc, playing an important role in building strong hair and collagen in the skin.

1 cup cashews, soaked 2 hours, drained, and rinsed
1 1/2 cups water
5-7 dates (honey or medjool), pitted
1/4 cup minced dill
2 tablespoons lemon juice
2 tablespoons olive oil

2 tablespoons flax seed oil
2 tablespoons miso
1 teaspoon onion powder
1/2 teaspoon black pepper
1/2 teaspoon garlic powder
1/2 teaspoon sea salt

Blend the cashews, dates, and water until smooth. Blend in the lemon juice, oils, miso, spices, and salt. Pulse in the minced dill. Serve immediately or refrigerate in an airtight container up to 3 days. **MAKES OVER 3 CUPS**

Citrus and Sesame Dressing

The tingling sensation of the taste of fresh citrus juices is a reminder that their fruit acids and vitamin C prevent age spots and wrinkles, keeping the skin youthful and luminous.

1 cup cubed oranges, deseeded
1 cup orange juice
1/2 cup lemon juice
1/4 cup honey or agave nectar
1/4 cup water
1/4 cup minced cilantro or parsley
3 tablespoons miso
2 tablespoons grated ginger

2 tablespoons liquid aminos or natural soy sauce
2 tablespoons olive oil
2 tablespoons white sesame seeds
1 tablespoon flax seed oil
2 teaspoons sesame oil
1/4 teaspoon onion powder
1/4 teaspoon sea salt

Use a lemon press or handheld juicer to make the citrus juices. Setting aside the minced cilantro, blend all the ingredients together until smooth. Pulse in the cilantro. Serve immediately or refrigerate in an airtight container up to 3 days. **MAKES ABOUT 4 CUPS**

Creamy Cashew Dill Dressing

with *Jewelry for the Dinner Table* by Jennifer

Nutty Garlic Parmesan Topping

Flax seeds provide a rich source of Omega 3 fatty acids and fiber, keeping the skin hydrated and smooth.

1 cup macadamia nuts
1 cup almonds
1/4 cup flax seeds

1/4 cup nutritional yeast
3 cloves garlic
1 1/2 teaspoons sea salt

Serving Suggestion
Add this topping to a soup or salad. This recipe can also be a topping for the *Spinach and Pumpkin Seed Manicotti* (see recipe page 77).

In a dry blender, grind the flax seeds to form a flour consistency and add to a bowl along with the nutritional yeast. Pulse the remaining ingredients in the blender one cup at a time until a crumbly texture is formed. Stop the blender to loosen the mixture with a rubber spatula as needed. Mix all ingredients together. Serve immediately or refrigerate in an airtight container up to 2 weeks. **MAKES OVER 2 CUPS**

Peppery Spice Sunflower Ranch

Sunflower seeds are plentiful in antioxidants for healthy skin.

1 cup sunflower seeds, soaked 2 hours, drained, and rinsed
1/2 cup almonds, soaked 8 hours, drained, and rinsed
1/2 cup chopped red bell peppers, deseeded
2 cups water
3 tablespoons apple cider vinegar

2 tablespoons honey or agave nectar
2 tablespoons olive oil
2 teaspoons onion powder
1 teaspoon black pepper
1 teaspoon white pepper
1/2 teaspoon cayenne
1/2 teaspoon sea salt

Blend the sunflower seeds, almonds, and water until smooth. Blend in the remaining ingredients. Serve immediately or refrigerate in an airtight container up to 3 days. **MAKES OVER 4 CUPS**

Asian Miso-Date Dressing

Dates are a skin beauty food. They also support digestion and relieve constipation.

1 cup orange juice
1/2 cup dates (honey or medjool), pitted and packed
2 tablespoons miso
1 tablespoon honey or agave nectar
1 tablespoon liquid aminos or natural soy sauce

1 tablespoon minced cilantro or parsley
1 tablespoon white sesame seeds + 1 tablespoon white sesame seeds
2 teaspoons sesame oil
1 teaspoon onion powder
1/2 teaspoon black pepper
1/2 teaspoon garlic powder

Use a lemon press or handheld juicer to make the orange juice. Setting aside 1 tablespoon sesame seeds and the minced cilantro, blend all the ingredients together until smooth. Pulse in the sesame seeds and cilantro. Do not over blend. Serve immediately or refrigerate in an airtight container up to 3 days. **MAKES ABOUT 2 CUPS**

Creamy Herbed Cucumber Salad

Fresh cucumbers are an inexpensive beauty food as they decrease puffy eyes and smooth out facial lines. Leave the peel on for extra silicon.

6 cups sliced cucumbers
1/2 cup cashews, soaked 2 hours, drained, and rinsed
1/3 cup water
1/4 cup nutritional yeast
1/4 cup minced dill

2 tablespoons minced parsley
1 tablespoon miso
1/4 teaspoon garlic powder
1/4 teaspoon white pepper
1/4 teaspoon sea salt
1 pinch nutmeg

Set aside the sliced cucumbers in a bowl. Blend the cashews and water until smooth. Blend in the nutritional yeast, miso, spices, and salt. Pulse in the dill and parsley. Do not over blend. Fold the mixture in with the cucumbers. Serve immediately. **SERVES 6 TO 8**

Spinach Pecan Salad with Blueberry-Date Dressing

The antioxidants in blueberries and citrus fruits counter toxins, keeping the skin luminous and firm.

SALAD
1 pound spinach
3/4 cup pecans
1/2 cup blueberries

1/2 cup finely chopped dates (honey or medjool), pitted and packed

DRESSING
1/2 cup dates (honey or medjool), pitted and packed
1/2 cup blueberries
3 tablespoons lemon juice
3 tablespoons olive oil

2 tablespoons lime juice
1 tablespoon liquid aminos or natural soy sauce
1 tablespoon olive oil or flax seed oil
1/4 teaspoon sea salt

Use a lemon press or handheld juicer to make the citrus juices. Blend all the dressing ingredients together until smooth. Drizzle the dressing over the spinach and top with the pecans, dates, and blueberries. Refrigerate the dressing in an airtight container up to 3 days. **SERVES 4**

Spinach Pecan Salad with
Blueberry-Date Dressing

Pickled Sesame Cabbage

Cabbage has powerful antioxidants that support detoxification in the liver. A healthy liver aids in keeping the bloodstream clean, preventing dull, blemished skin.

8 cups thinly sliced cabbage
(about 1 medium head)
1 large carrot, julienned
(matchstick slices)
1 large cucumber, thinly sliced
2 tablespoons apple cider vinegar

1 large red bell pepper, julienned
(matchstick slices)
1/2 cup white sesame seeds, soaked 2
hours, drained, and rinsed
2 teaspoons sesame oil
2 teaspoons sea salt

In a large glass bowl, add the cabbage, carrots, bell pepper, and salt. Massage with hands until the liquid releases. Wait 10 minutes and massage again. Fold in the cucumbers with the remaining ingredients. This recipe can be served immediately or fermented.

To ferment, the liquid must be enough to cover the vegetables. Contents can ferment in a glass bowl or transferred to a large glass jar. Place a weight, such as a smaller jar filled with water over the cabbage mixture. Cover with a towel and let sit in a cool, dark place for 3 days and up to 10 days, depending on the desired level of pickling. Refrigerate in a sealed glass jar up to1 month. **SERVES 8 TO 10**

Pickled Sesame Cabbage

SIDES

Spicy Fusion Guacamole

Whether eaten or applied directly to the skin, avocados are one of the finest moisturizers with their rich source of healthy fat and phytonutrients.

3 medium avocados, ripe
1/2 cup finely diced red bell peppers, deseeded
2 tablespoons miso
1 tablespoon lemon juice

1/4 teaspoon cayenne
1/4 teaspoon garlic powder
1/4 teaspoon white pepper
1 pinch sea salt

With a fork, mash all the ingredients together until smooth. Serve immediately or refrigerate in an airtight container up to 2 days. **MAKES ABOUT 2 CUPS**

Zesty Cauliflower Pilaf

Cauliflower is a sulfur-rich food, supporting hair, skin, and nails as well as healing scar tissue. Cauliflower is best digested when eaten with natural fats, such as the olive oil and sunflower seeds in this recipe.

6 cups finely chopped cauliflower (about 1 medium head)
1 cup finely diced celery with leaves
1/2 cup sunflower seeds, soaked 2 hours, drained, and rinsed

1/4 cup minced onions
1/4 cup olive oil
2 tablespoons lemon juice
1 tablespoon lemon zest
1/2 teaspoon sea salt

Place the cauliflower and salt in a large bowl. Massage the salt into the cauliflower until the mixture softens. Fold in the remaining ingredients. Serve immediately or refrigerate in an airtight container up to 3 days. **SERVES 6 TO 8**

Zesty Cauliflower Pilaf

Onion Sour Cream

Onions are a good source of silicon and MSM (methyl-sulfonyl-methane), strengthening hair, skin, and nails.

2 cups cashews, soaked 2 hours,
drained, and rinsed
1 cup water
1/4 cup chopped onions
1 tablespoon lemon juice

2 teaspoons miso
1 teaspoon onion powder
1/4 teaspoon white pepper
1/4 teaspoon sea salt

Serving Suggestion
Use as a dip or salad dressing. This recipe is also a topping for the *Tomato Ginger Bisque* (see recipe page 44).

Blend the cashews and water until smooth. Blend in the remaining ingredients and then pour the mixture into a glass bowl or jar. This recipe can be served immediately or be fermented. To ferment, cover the sour cream with a breathable towel and let sit for 8 to 12 hours at room temperature and out of direct sunlight. Refrigerate in an airtight container up to 5 days. **MAKES OVER 3 CUPS**

Breaded Avocado Wedges

The healthy fats in avocado and flax seeds are internal hydrators and external moisturizers.

3 medium avocados
1/4 cup ground flax seeds
1/4 cup nutritional yeast
2 tablespoons apple cider vinegar

1 teaspoon onion powder
3/4 teaspoon chili powder
1/2 teaspoon sea salt
1/4 teaspoon cayenne

For the breading, blend the flax seeds to form a flour consistency and place in a bowl. Add the nutritional yeast, onion powder, chili powder, cayenne, and salt to the bowl and combine. Slice the avocados in half and remove the pit. With the peel still on, slice the avocado halves into 1/4 inch long wedges. Remove the peel and dip each wedge into the apple cider vinegar and then coat each wedge with the breading. Serve immediately. **SERVES 4 TO 6**

Breaded Avocado Wedges

Lemon Butter Corn

Yellow sweet corn is a good source of antioxidants, including lutein, which keeps eyes sparkling.

4 cups sweet corn kernels
1 cup finely diced celery
2 tablespoons lemon juice
2 tablespoons olive oil

2 teaspoons lemon zest
1/4 teaspoon black pepper
1/4 teaspoon sea salt

GARNISHES
2 tablespoons finely diced green onions
Sliced lemon halves

Mix all the ingredients together in a bowl. Garnish with green onions and lemon. Serve immediately or refrigerate in an airtight container up to 3 days.
SERVES 4 TO 6

American-Style Creamed Corn

Sweet corn keeps skin youthful with its abundant source of antioxidants.

3 cups sweet corn kernels + 1/4 cup
sweet corn kernels
1/2 cup cashews, soaked 2 hours,
drained, and rinsed

1/2 cup water
1 teaspoon honey or agave nectar
1/4 teaspoon black pepper
1/4 teaspoon sea salt

Set aside 3 cups kernels in a medium bowl. Blend the cashews and water until smooth. Add in the remaining 1/4 cup kernels, honey, black pepper, and salt until smooth. Pour the blended mixture into the bowl of kernels and gently fold in. Serve immediately or refrigerate in an airtight container up to 2 days.
SERVES 4 TO 6

Lemon Butter Corn

Zucchini and Pumpkin Seed Hummus

The healthy fat in pumpkin seeds gives the skin a clear and luminous complexion. They also help prevent inflammation.

1 1/2 cups chopped zucchini
1 cup pumpkin seeds, soaked 4 to 6 hours, drained, and rinsed
3/4 cup cashews, soaked 2 hours, drained, and rinsed
2 dates (red/jujube, honey, or medjool) soaked in 1/2 cup water (do not drain)
1/2 cup nutritional yeast
1/4 cup minced parsley

2 tablespoons apple cider vinegar
2 tablespoons lemon juice
2 tablespoons miso
2 tablespoons olive oil
2 garlic cloves
2 teaspoons garlic powder
1/2 teaspoon sea salt
1/4 teaspoon spirulina (optional)

GARNISHES
1 tablespoon olive oil
Sprigs of parsley

Blend the pumpkin seeds, cashews, dates, 1/2 cup soaking water, and lemon juice until smooth. Blend in the zucchini, olive oil, miso, garlic cloves, garlic powder, salt, and spirulina. Pour the thick mixture into a bowl and fold in the nutritional yeast and minced parsley. Transfer the mixture into a serving bowl and drizzle olive oil over the top and garnish with a sprig or two of parsley. Serve immediately or refrigerate in an airtight container up to 3 days. **MAKES ABOUT 4 CUPS**

Berry Medley

This bowl of antioxidants rejuvenates the skin back to life.

2 cups blueberries
2 cups raspberries

2 cups strawberries

Serving Suggestion
Serve with *Cashew Whip Cream* (see recipe page 89). For a thinner, half-and-half cream consistency, use the *Sweet Almond and Red Date Cream* (see recipe page 30).

Serve immediately or refrigerate in an airtight container up to 3 days. **SERVES 6 TO 8**

Sweet and Spicy Red Pepper Mayo

The fermented properties in miso are known for their anti-aging benefits as well as provide the digestive tract beneficial bacteria. This recipe makes a good dip or salad topping.

1 cup chopped red bell peppers,
deseeded
1/2 cup cashews, soaked 2 hours,
drained, and rinsed
1/2 cup water
2 tablespoons honey or agave nectar

2 tablespoons miso
2 tablespoons white sesame seeds
1/2 teaspoon sesame oil
1/2 teaspoon sea salt
1/8 teaspoon cayenne

Serving Suggestion
Serve as a topping for the *Marinated Sesame and Mushroom Sushi Rolls* (see recipe page 74).

Blend the cashews and water until smooth. Add the remaining ingredients and blend again. Serve immediately or refrigerate in an airtight container up to 4 days.
MAKES OVER 2 CUPS

Asian Shells with Honey Ginger Glaze

Rich in antioxidants and sulfur, red cabbage is known for its anti-inflammatory properties and keeping skin youthful.

SHELLS
8-10 red cabbage leaves

SALAD
2 cups diced pears
1 cup cherry tomato halves
1 cup diced cucumbers

1/2 cup diced celery
1/2 cup sweet corn kernels

GLAZE
2 tablespoons honey or agave nectar
2 teaspoons grated ginger

1/2 teaspoon sea salt
1 pinch cayenne

GARNISHES
3/4 cup cashews
Celery leaves
Cayenne

With kitchen scissors shape the cabbage leaves into small rounds and set aside. Add the salad contents to a bowl and fold in the glaze. Add 1/2 cup or more salad to each cabbage shell. Garnish each salad shell with cashews, celery leaves, and a pinch of cayenne. Serve immediately or refrigerate in an airtight container up to 2 days. **SERVES 8 TO 10**

Asian Shells with Honey Ginger Glaze

ENTRÉES

Zucchini Fettuccini with Pumpkin Seed Pesto

The zinc along with the enzymatic properties in pumpkin seeds beautify the complexion and improve acne-prone skin.

NOODLES
6 cups zucchini noodles (about 4 medium zucchinis)
1/4 teaspoon sea salt

PESTO
2 cups minced basil
3/4 cup pumpkin seeds
1/2 cup minced parsley
2 tablespoons flax seed oil
2 tablespoons nutritional yeast
2 tablespoons olive oil
1 tablespoon miso
1 teaspoon minced garlic
1/4 teaspoon sea salt

GARNISHES
Basil leaves
2 tablespoons pumpkin seeds

To make the noodles, use a vegetable peeler to form fettuccini-shaped noodles. Coat the noodles with salt and place them in a strainer lined with a paper towel. Set aside for 10 minutes and then gently pat the noodles with a paper towel to soak up excess water.

To make the pesto, pulse the pumpkin seeds in a dry blender to form a crumbly mixture. Add the crumbled pumpkin seeds to a bowl along with the rest of the ingredients. Using a fork, mash the contents together to form a paste.

In a large bowl, gently fold the pesto in with the zucchini, making sure all the noodles are coated. Garnish the dish with basil leaves and pumpkin seeds. Serve immediately or refrigerate in an airtight container up to 2 days. **SERVES 6**

Pumpkin Seed and Sundried Tomato Pâté Wraps

Collard greens, along with many leafy greens, are low calorie and nutrient-dense beauty foods.

WRAPS
4-6 large collard green leaves (or any flat leaves)

FILLING
2 cups pumpkin seeds
1/2 cup finely diced sundried tomatoes
1/2 cup water
1/4 cup lemon juice

2 tablespoons miso
1/2 teaspoon black pepper
1/4 teaspoon sea salt

To prepare the wraps, lay the leaves, shiny side down and remove the stems and veins. The more of the vein removed the easier the leaf will roll.

To make the filling, in a dry blender pulse the pumpkin seeds to form a crumbly mixture. In a bowl, mash together the crumbled pumpkin seeds with the remaining ingredients.

To assemble, lay one leaf shiny side down. Starting at the base of the leaf, layer a horizontal row of filling and roll. With a serrated knife, slice the rolls in half. **MAKES 4 TO 6 WRAPS**

Marinated Sesame and Mushroom Sushi Rolls

Sea vegetables are a true beauty food, containing superior sources of trace minerals and detoxification properties.

SUSHI CONTENTS
10 nori seaweed sheets
5 cups alfalfa or broccoli sprouts
3 medium avocados, ripe, thinly sliced
1 large carrot, julienned (matchstick slices)
1 large cucumber, thinly sliced
1 large red or yellow bell pepper, julienned (matchstick slices)

MUSHROOMS
4 cups thinly sliced mushrooms (button, shiitake, etc.)
1/2 cup liquid aminos or natural soy sauce
2 tablespoons black sesame seeds
2 tablespoons grated ginger
1 tablespoon honey or agave nectar
2 teaspoons sesame oil
1/2 teaspoon sea salt

Serving Suggestion
Top with *Sweet and Spicy Red Pepper Mayo* (see recipe page 69).

To marinate the mushrooms, combine the mushrooms with the marinating ingredients in a bowl. Let stand for at least 20 minutes. Remove the mushrooms from the bowl, and gently squeeze out the juice. This leftover juice is the sesame-flavored soy sauce for the sushi.

To make the sushi, place a nori sheet, shiny side down, on a bamboo sushi mat. On the side closest to you, layer a horizontal row of sprouts, two-inches wide and one-half inch away from the nori sheet's edge. On top of the sprouts, layer narrow strips of the vegetables, including the mushrooms. Starting with the side closest to you, use your thumbs to flip the nori sheet over the contents. Keep the contents firm by using the bamboo mat to shape the roll, sliding it over and across the top of the sushi roll. Before the roll is complete, dab a little bit of warm water along the remaining nori's edge to seal the roll. Use a serrated knife to slice the sushi. Slice the roll in half and then slice the halves in half two more times to make 8 sushi pieces. Serve immediately. **MAKES 10 ROLLS**

Marinated Sesame and Mushroom Sushi Rolls

with Sweet and Spicy Red Pepper Mayo
and Sesame-flavored Soy Sauce

**Spinach and Pumpkin
Seed Manicotti**

Spinach and Pumpkin Seed Manicotti

Spinach boasts a high amount of lutein, keeping eyes bright and vibrant.

NOODLES
4-6 medium zucchinis
1/4 teaspoon sea salt

FILLING
2 cups spinach, packed
1 cup zucchini peels (optional)
3/4 cup pumpkin seeds, soaked 4 to 6 hours, drained, and rinsed
1/4 cup water
1/4 cup lemon juice

1/4 cup nutritional yeast
1 tablespoon miso
1 teaspoon onion powder
1 clove garlic
1/2 teaspoon garlic powder
1/2 teaspoon sea salt

TOPPINGS
2 cups chopped tomatoes
1/2 cup sundried tomatoes soaked in 1/2 cup water (do not drain)
2 tablespoons nutritional yeast
1 tablespoon minced basil

1 tablespoon olive oil
1/2 teaspoon onion powder
1/4 teaspoon garlic powder
1/4 teaspoon sea salt

Serving Suggestion
Top with *Nutty Garlic Parmesan Topping* (see recipe page 56).

To make the noodles, thinly slice the zucchinis length-wise into long, wide noodles. The thinner the noodle the easier it will roll. Coat the noodles with salt and place them in a strainer lined with a paper towel. Set aside for 10 minutes and then gently pat the noodles with a paper towel to soak up excess water.

To make the filling, blend the pumpkin seeds, water, and lemon juice until smooth. Blend in the spinach, zucchini peels, and garlic cloves until smooth, stopping the blender several times to scrape down the sides with a rubber spatula. A little water may need to be added, but using the rubber spatula to keep the mixture blending is the best result for a thicker filling. Pour the filling into a bowl and stir in the remaining dry ingredients.

To make the topping, soak the sundried tomatoes in the water for at least 10 minutes. Blend the sundried tomatoes, 1/2 cup soaking water, and tomatoes until smooth. Pour the mixture into a bowl and add in the remaining ingredients. To avoid this topping from getting watery, pour the mixture into a strainer and let sit 5 minutes to drain any excess water.

To assemble, on a bamboo sushi mat, place four zucchini noodles vertically and overlapping one another by 1/2 inch. On the side closest to you, layer on a horizontal row of filling. To roll, use your thumbs to flip the zucchini sheet over the filling, sliding the bamboo sheet over and across the top until a manicotti is formed. Add the tomato topping over the top of 2 manicottis with some *Nutty Garlic Parmesan Topping* if desired. Serve immediately or store contents individually up to 3 days. **SERVES 4 TO 6**

Stuffed Tomatoes

Tomatoes act as skin preservers, fighting dullness and large pores. In addition, the lycopene in tomatoes is a powerful antioxidant and natural sunscreen for the skin.

BOWLS
6-8 large tomatoes

FILLING
1 cup finely diced cauliflower
1 cup walnuts
3/4 cup finely diced mushrooms
(button, shiitake, etc.)
1/2 cup minced onions
1/4 cup minced parsley
2 tablespoons liquid aminos or natural

soy sauce
2 teaspoons olive oil
1 teaspoon flax seed oil
1/2 teaspoon black pepper
1/2 teaspoon onion powder
1/2 teaspoon sea salt
1 pinch cayenne

Serving Suggestion
Top with *Onion Sour Cream* (see recipe page 64).

GARNISH
Sprigs of parsley

For the filling, in a dry blender pulse the walnuts into a crumbly mixture and add to a large bowl along with the remaining ingredients and combine well.

To assemble, cut the tomato tops off and scoop out the insides. Stuff each tomato with the filling. Garnish by adding a dollop of the *Onion Sour Cream*. Another option is to pipe on the sour cream with a piping bag, a squeeze bottle, or plastic sealed bag with a small incision made at the bottom corner. Garnish each tomato with a sprig of parsley. **MAKES 6 TO 8 STUFFED TOMATOES**

Tacos with Ground Walnut and Red Bell Pepper

Walnuts promote a smooth complexion and vibrant skin with their high mineral content and Omega 3 fatty acids.

SHELLS
6-8 large romaine leaves

FILLING
2 cups walnuts
1 cup minced mushrooms, (button, shiitake, etc.)
1/2 cup finely diced red bell peppers
2 tablespoons flax seeds
2 tablespoons minced cilantro
1 tablespoon apple cider vinegar
1 tablespoon liquid aminos or natural

soy sauce
1/2 teaspoon chili powder
1/2 teaspoon cumin
1/2 teaspoon onion powder
1/4 teaspoon garlic powder
1/4 teaspoon cayenne
1/4 teaspoon sea salt

Serving Suggestion
Top with *Onion Sour Cream* (see recipe page 64).

For the taco shells, fold the romaine leaves in half so the stem is the base of the taco. If desired, cut each folded leaf so they are 4 inches long.

For the filling, in a dry blender pulse the flax seeds into a flour consistency and set aside in a large bowl. Add the walnuts to the blender and pulse until a crumbly texture is formed, stopping the blender to loosen the mixture with a rubber spatula as needed. Add the crumbled walnut mixture and the remaining ingredients to the bowl with the ground flax and mix well.

To assemble, add about 1/2 cup ground filling to each lettuce shell. Garnish by adding a dollop of the *Onion Sour Cream*. Another option is to pipe on the sour cream with a piping bag, a squeeze bottle, or plastic sealed bag with a small incision made at the bottom corner. Serve immediately or store contents individually up to 3 days. **MAKES 6 TO 8 TACOS**

Tacos with Ground Walnut and Red Bell Pepper

Tomato, Mushroom, and Spinach-Pesto Torte

Sunflower seeds boast a rich source of vitamin E, slowing down the aging process and preventing age spots.

LAYERS
2 large tomatoes, sliced
1/2 pound spinach

MUSHROOMS
4 cups thinly sliced mushrooms
2 teaspoons olive oil

1/2 teaspoon black pepper
1/2 teaspoon sea salt

PESTO
3/4 cup minced spinach
1/2 cup sunflower seeds, soaked 2 hours, drained, and rinsed
2 tablespoons nutritional yeast
1 tablespoon miso

1 tablespoon olive oil
1/2 teaspoon black pepper
1/2 teaspoon minced garlic
1/2 teaspoon sea salt

To prepare the layers, place the tomato slices on a paper towel to soak up excess water and remove the spinach stems.

To marinate the mushrooms, combine the marinating ingredients in a bowl and let stand for at least 20 minutes. Gently squeeze the mushrooms and discard the excess water. Place the mushrooms on a paper towel before making the pesto.

To make the pesto, pulse the sunflower seeds in a dry blender to form a crumbly mixture. Add the crumbled sunflower seeds to a bowl along with the rest of the ingredients. Using a fork, mash the contents together to form a paste.

To assemble, stack the contents in the order of tomato, pesto, mushrooms, spinach, pesto, and tomato. **MAKES 4 TO 6 TORTES**

Chinese Instant Noodles

Instant noodles literally mean "convenient noodles" in Chinese. This veggie version offers beauty in a bowl.

NOODLES
4 medium zucchinis

BROTH
3 cups water
1/2 cup chopped mushrooms (button, shiitake, etc.)
1 teaspoon miso

1 teaspoon sesame oil
1/2 teaspoon sea salt
1/4 teaspoon black pepper
1/4 teaspoon white pepper

TOPPING
1/4 cup finely diced carrots
1/4 cup finely diced celery
1/4 cup finely diced green onion

1/4 cup finely diced red or yellow bell peppers

To make the noodles, use a vegetable peeler or a spiral slicer. Place the noodles in serving bowls.

To make the broth, blend the ingredients together until smooth. Cool, warm, or hot water can be used for this recipe.

To assemble, pour broth into each bowl of noodles. Top each bowl with the finely diced vegetables. **SERVES 4 TO 6**

Chinese Instant Noodles

Collard Green Dolmas

The high levels of antioxidants in cauliflower protect against free radical damage, reducing the signs of aging.

WRAPS
12-18 collard green leaves (or any flat leaves)

MARINADE
1/4 cup olive oil
1 tablespoon lemon juice
2 teaspoons honey or agave nectar
1 teaspoon minced garlic
1 teaspoon sea salt

FILLING
2 cups minced mushrooms
2 cups minced cauliflower
1/2 cup macadamia nuts
1/2 cup finely diced dates or raisins
1/2 cup minced onions
2 tablespoons flax seeds
2 tablespoons lemon juice
2 tablespoons liquid aminos or natural
soy sauce
2 tablespoons minced peppermint
1 tablespoon olive oil
1 teaspoon black pepper
3/4 teaspoon sea salt
1/4 teaspoon cinnamon
1/4 teaspoon nutmeg

To prepare the wraps, lay the leaves, shiny side down and remove the stems and veins. The more of the vein removed the easier the leaf will roll. In a shallow pan marinate the leaves in the liquid for at least 1 hour.

For the filling, in a dry blender pulse the flax seeds into a flour consistency and set aside in a large bowl. Then pulse the macadamia nuts into a crumbly mixture and add to the same bowl. Combine all the ingredients together.

To assemble, place a leaf shiny side down. Add a spoonful or two of the filling, depending on the leaf's size, at the base. Roll the base of the leaf over the mixture and then fold in the sides before rolling the rest of the way.

If the dolmas start to unfold, use a toothpick to hold them together and remove before serving. Another option is to wrap each dolma in plastic wrap and remove before serving. **MAKES 12 TO 18 DOLMAS**

Collard Green Dolmas

Almond & Sunflower Seed Pâté Sushi Rolls

Nori and celery provide ample amounts of sodium. Unlike table salt (sodium chloride), natural sodium distributes water evenly throughout the body, keeping skin hydrated.

WRAPS
6 nori seaweed sheets

FILLING
1 cup almonds
1 cup sunflower seeds
1/2 cup water

1/2 cup thinly sliced celery
1/4 cup lemon juice
1/4 teaspoon black pepper

In a dry blender, pulse the almonds and sunflower seeds one cup at a time in a blender to form a crumbly mixture. Combine all the ingredients together in a bowl and mix thoroughly.

To make the sushi, place a nori sheet, shiny side down, on a bamboo sushi mat. On the side closest to you, layer a horizontal row of filling one-half inch away from the nori sheet's edge. Starting with the side closest to you, use your thumbs to flip the nori sheet over the contents. Keep the contents firm by using the bamboo mat to shape the roll, sliding it over and across the top of the sushi roll. Before the roll is complete, dab a little bit of warm water along the remaining nori's edge to seal the roll. Use a serrated knife to slice the sushi. Slice the roll in half one more time to make 4 sushi pieces. Serve immediately. **MAKES 6 ROLLS**

DESSERTS

Cashew Whip Cream

Cashews play an important role in beauty, giving hair and skin their natural pigmentation due to its rich copper content.

1 cup cashews, soaked 2 hours, drained, and rinsed
1/2 cup water
2 teaspoons coconut oil

1 teaspoon honey or agave nectar
1/2 teaspoon vanilla extract
1 pinch sea salt

Blend the cashews and water until smooth. Blend in the remaining ingredients. Serve immediately or refrigerate in an airtight container up to 3 days. **MAKES OVER 1 CUP**

Peppermint Chocolate Mousse

Peppermint's antiseptic and therapeutic properties cleanse and purify the skin.

MOUSSE
3 cups *Almond Milk* (see recipe page 26)
3 medium avocados, ripe
3/4 cup cacao or carob powder
1/3 cup honey or agave nectar
1/2 cup coconut oil
2 teaspoons vanilla extract

1/4 teaspoon cinnamon
1/8 teaspoon sea salt
1 drop peppermint oil extract
1 pinch nutmeg
1 pinch spirulina

MINT TOPPING
1 cup "green" mousse topping

GARNISH
Sprigs of peppermint

To start the mousse, set aside the cacao, cinnamon, nutmeg, and peppermint oil extract and blend all the ingredients together until smooth. Do not over blend the avocados. Pour 1 cup mousse in a bowl and set aside. This is the "green" mint topping.

To finish the mousse, add the cacao, cinnamon, nutmeg, and peppermint oil extract to the remaining mousse in the blender and whirl again. To add the peppermint oil extract, dip a clean toothpick in the oil and add one drop from the toothpick. For a stronger mint flavor, repeat the step with a clean toothpick. Pour the mousse into serving bowls or glasses and refrigerate for at least 20 minutes. Add a dollop of the mint topping and garnish with a sprig of peppermint. Serve or refrigerate in an airtight container up to 2 days. **SERVES 6 TO 8**

Peppermint Chocolate Mousse

Strawberry Tart with a Macadamia Nut Crust

Strawberries are abundant in silicon, strengthening the hair, skin, and nails.

CRUST
1 1/2 cups macadamia nuts
1 cup cashews
1 cup coconut flour*

1/3 cup honey or agave nectar
1/8 teaspoon sea salt

FILLING
5 cups sliced strawberries
2 tablespoons honey or agave nectar
2 tablespoons lemon juice

1 tablespoon lime juice
2 teaspoons vanilla extract
1 pinch sea salt

GARNISH
Sprigs of peppermint

To make the crust, in a dry blender pulse the dry ingredients one cup at a time to form a crumbly mixture. Stop the blender to loosen the mixture with a rubber spatula as needed. Pour the mixture into a bowl. Add the honey and gently combine the mixture to form a light crumble, working the mixture through the fingers. Pour the crumble in a 9-inch tart pan, pie plate, or spring form pan lined with parchment paper. Spread the crumble evenly with more content around the rim to form an edge. Press the mixture down with the fingers to form a firm layer of crust.

To make the filling, gently fold all the ingredients together until the strawberries are coated. Pour the filling into the crust. Garnish with sprigs of peppermint. Serve immediately or refrigerate in an airtight container up to 2 days. **MAKES 1 9-INCH TART**

*If coconut shreds are used, pulse the shreds in a dry blender to form a flour consistency.

Lime Mousse with Mango Coulis

Coconut oil makes a topical moisturizer for the skin and hair. It can also be used as a natural make-up remover.

MOUSSE
1 1/2 cups *Pumpkin Seed Milk* (see recipe page 26)
2 medium avocados, ripe
1/2 cup coconut oil
1/3 cup honey or agave nectar

1/3 cup lemon juice
1/3 cup lime juice
1 teaspoon lime zest
1/4 teaspoon sea salt
1 pinch spirulina or chlorella

COULIS
2 cups cubed or sliced mangos, fresh or frozen
2 tablespoons lemon juice

1/3 cup dates (honey or medjool), soaked 15 minutes and drained

GARNISH
Sliced lime halves

To make the mousse, blend the pumpkin seed milk, coconut oil, honey, citrus juices, lime zest, salt, and spirulina until smooth. Blend in the avocados. Do not over blend. Pour the mousse into serving bowls or glasses and refrigerate for at least 20 minutes.

To make the coulis, blend all the ingredients together until smooth. Top the mousse with a dollop of coulis and garnish with a half slice lime. Serve or refrigerate in an airtight container up to 2 days. **SERVES 6**

Pistachio Peppermint Pudding

The vitamin E in pistachios is essential for skin health and protects against UV radiation damage.

2 cups *Almond Milk* (see recipe page 26)
3 medium avocados, ripe
3/4 cup pistachios*
1/2 cup honey or agave nectar
1 tablespoon minced peppermint

2 teaspoons vanilla extract
1/8 teaspoon sea salt
1 drop peppermint oil extract
1 pinch spirulina or chlorella

Setting the pistachios and avocados aside, blend the almond milk, honey, peppermint leaves, vanilla, spirulina, and salt until smooth. Blend in the avocados and peppermint oil extract. Do not over blend. To add the peppermint oil extract, dip a clean toothpick in the oil and add one drop from the toothpick. For a stronger mint flavor, repeat the step with a clean toothpick. Pulse in the pistachios until each pistachio is broken into about three or four pieces. Serve immediately or refrigerate in an airtight container up to 2 days. **SERVES 4 TO 6**

*If salted pistachios are used omit the salt in this recipe.

Pistachio Peppermint Pudding

Frozen Chocolate Mousse Cake

Frozen Chocolate Mousse Cake

Both cacao and carob are rich in antioxidants, helping to repair the body of free radical damage, which causes aging. Sometimes I use half cacao and half carob.

CRUST
1 1/2 cups walnuts
1 cup coconut flour*
3/4 cup cacao or carob powder

1/4 cup honey or agave nectar
2 tablespoons coconut oil
1/8 teaspoon sea salt

FILLING
2 cups cashews, soaked 2 hours, drained, and rinsed
1 1/2 cups *Almond Milk* (see recipe page 26)
1 cup cacao or carob powder
3/4 cup dates (honey or medjool), pitted

and packed
1/2 cup maple syrup
1/3 cup coconut oil
2 teaspoons vanilla extract
1/4 teaspoon cinnamon
1 pinch sea salt

COULIS
2 cups strawberries, fresh or frozen
1 tablespoon honey or agave nectar

2-3 dates (honey or medjool), soaked 15 minutes and drained

Serving Suggestion
Top the entire cake with whole strawberries or *Cashew Whip Cream* (see recipe page 89).

To make the crust, in a dry blender pulse the walnuts and coconut flour one cup at a time to form a crumbly mixture. Stop the blender to loosen the mixture with a rubber spatula as needed. Pour the mixture into a bowl. Add the honey and coconut oil and gently combine the mixture to form a light crumble, working the mixture through the fingers. Pour the crumble in a 9-inch spring form pan lined with parchment paper. Spread the crumble out evenly and then press down with the fingers to form a firm layer of crust.

To make the filling, soak the dates in the almond milk for at least 15 minutes to soften. Then blend the almond milk, dates, cashews, and maple syrup together until smooth. While the blender is running, add the coconut oil and vanilla. Pour the thick mixture into a bowl and stir in the cacao powder, cinnamon, and salt. Pour the filling into the pan. Freeze at least 2 hours or overnight.

To make the coulis, blend the strawberries, dates, and honey until smooth.

Take the cake out of the freezer 20 minutes before serving. Garnish each slice with a dollop of strawberry coulis and *Cashew Whip Cream* if desired. Another option is to pipe on the coulis and *Cashew Whip Cream* with a piping bag, a squeeze bottle, or plastic sealed bag with a small incision made at the bottom corner. Serve or freeze in an airtight container up to 1 month. **MAKES 1 9-INCH CAKE**

*If coconut shreds are used, pulse the shreds in a dry blender to form a flour consistency.

Super Green Cacao Energy Balls

Cinnamon relieves dry skin and supports blood circulation.

2 cups sunflower seeds
1 1/2 cups raisins
1/2 cup sesame seeds
1/2 cup cacao or carob powder
1/4 cup honey or agave nectar

1 teaspoon young barley or wheatgrass powder
1 teaspoon spirulina or chlorella powder
1/8 teaspoon sea salt

COATING
2 tablespoons cacao or carob powder

In a dry blender pulse the sunflower seeds, raisins, and sesame seeds one cup at a time to form a crumbly mixture. Stop the blender to loosen the mixture with a rubber spatula as needed. As long as the raisins are broken up in two or three pieces is fine. Pour the mixture into a bowl with the remaining ingredients and combine. With the hands, roll about 1-inch balls and then roll in the cacao powder. Serve immediately or refrigerate in an airtight container up to 2 weeks. **MAKES 18 TO 20 BALLS**

Apple Pecan Crumble

Apples cleanse the digestive tract. The pectin in apples also helps remove heavy metals and radiation residues.

TOPPING
2 1/2 cups pecans
1/2 cup raisins
1 or 2 pinches sea salt

FILLING
5 cups finely diced apples
1 cup dates (honey or medjool), pitted
and packed
1/2 cup raisins
1/2 cup water
2 tablespoons maple syrup

1 tablespoon lemon juice
2 teaspoons vanilla extract
1 teaspoon cinnamon
1/2 teaspoon nutmeg
1 pinch sea salt

Serving Suggestion
Serve with *Cashew Whip Cream* (see recipe page 89).

To make the crumble, in a dry blender pulse the dry ingredients, including the raisins, one cup at a time to form a crumbly mixture. Stop the blender to loosen the mixture with a rubber spatula as needed. Pour the mixture into a bowl and set aside.

To make the filling, in another bowl combine the apples and lemon juice and set aside. Next, blend the dates, raisins, water, maple syrup, vanilla, spices, and salt until smooth. Fold the blended mixture into the apples. To assemble, spread the apple filling evenly into a 9-inch pie plate and then add the topping. Serve immediately or refrigerate in an airtight container up to 2 days. **MAKES 1 9-INCH PIE**

Chocolate Layered Cherry Cream Tart

Chocolate Layered Cherry Cream Tart

Cherries are sweet dispensers of antioxidants, known for their rich anti-aging benefits as well as preventing inflammation and arthritis.

CRUST
2 cups walnuts
3/4 cup nut or seed pulp (any kind)
3/4 cup coconut flour*
3/4 cup raisins
1 pinch sea salt

SAUCE
3/4 cup cacao or carob powder
3/4 cup coconut oil
1/3 cup maple syrup
1/2 teaspoon cinnamon
1/4 teaspoon nutmeg

FILLING
1 1/2 cups cashews, soaked 2 hours, drained, and rinsed
3/4 cup water
1 tablespoon maple syrup
1 teaspoon vanilla extract
1 pinch sea salt

TOPPING
2 1/2 cups pitted cherries, fresh or frozen

To make the crust, in a dry blender pulse the dry ingredients, including the raisins, one cup at a time to form a crumbly mixture. Stop the blender to loosen the mixture with a rubber spatula as needed. Pour the mixture into a bowl. Add the nut or seed pulp and gently combine the mixture to form a light crumble, working the mixture through the fingers. Pour the crumble in a 9-inch tart pan or spring form pan lined with parchment paper. Spread the mixture out evenly with more content around the rim to form an edge. Press down with the fingers to form a firm layer of crust.

To make the sauce, blend all ingredients together until smooth. Pour the sauce over the base of the crust. Place the chocolate-layered crust in the freezer for 10 minutes.

To make the filling, blend the cashews and water until smooth. Blend in the remaining ingredients. Pour the filling over the chocolate-layered crust. Place the whole or halved cherries on top. If the pitted cherries are whole, press them down half way into the filling. Place the tart in the freezer for at least 2 hours. Take out 20 minutes before serving. Serve or freeze in an airtight container up to 1 month. **MAKES 1 9-INCH TART**

*If coconut shreds are used, pulse the shreds in a dry blender to form a flour consistency.

Pecan Truffles

Pecans boast a buttery-rich flavor and an abundant source of vitamin E, promoting skin health and slowing down the aging process.

2 cups pecans
1 1/2 cups cashews
1 cup cacao or carob powder
1 tablespoon vanilla

1/4 cup coconut oil
1/4 cup honey or agave nectar
1/4 teaspoon cinnamon
1/4 teaspoon sea salt

COATINGS
Cacao powder
Carob powder
Coconut flour
Maca powder

Orange peel, grated
Pecans, finely chopped
Pecan halves

In a dry blender pulse the pecans and cashews one cup at a time to form a flour consistency. Stop the blender to loosen the mixture with a rubber spatula as needed. Pour the mixture into a bowl with the remaining ingredients and combine. With the hands, roll about 1-inch balls and then roll in the desired coatings. Serve immediately or refrigerate in an airtight container up to 2 weeks. **MAKES 24 TO 30 TRUFFLES**

Pecan Truffles

Frosted Pumpkin Seed and Date Balls

Lemons help dull skin return to a natural glow. They also reduce blackheads and tighten pores.

2 cups pumpkin seeds
1 1/2 cups finely diced dates* (honey or medjool)
1 cup coconut flour*

1/4 cup lemon juice
1/4 cup maple syrup
2 tablespoons maca powder
1/8 teaspoon sea salt

COATING
1/4 cup coconut flour

In a dry blender pulse the pumpkin seeds one cup at a time to form a crumbly mixture. Stop the blender to loosen the mixture with a rubber spatula as needed. Pour the mixture into a bowl with the remaining ingredients and combine. With the hands, roll about 1-inch balls and then roll in the coconut flour. Serve immediately or refrigerate in an airtight container up to 2 weeks. **MAKES 18 TO 20 BALLS**

*If dates are hard, pulse the pitted dates in the blender until each date is broken up in three or four pieces.

*If coconut shreds are used, pulse the shreds in a dry blender to form a flour consistency.

Super Green Cacao Energy and
Frosted Pumpkin Seed
and Date Balls

LIFESTYLE TIPS & BEAUTY RECIPES

Detoxification through Raw Foods

The human body is created to remove waste. A healthy colon produces good bacteria and microorganisms called flora. However, because of increasing amounts of toxicity in food, water, and air, the body experiences difficulty keeping up with good housecleaning. Excreting toxins through the bowels, sweat glands, and skin is part of the removal system known as detoxification.

When I transitioned to eating raw, a surge of energy, lightness, and wellbeing overcame me. One could say I was high on raw. At the same time, my body experienced deep cleaning as it removed years of accumulated toxins, including heavy metals and chemicals stored in fat and muscle tissue.

Detoxing through the skin via acne, rashes, and other outbreaks is not the most efficient way the body cleanses—it's certainly not the most attractive either. These outward imperfections are signs the digestive tract cannot keep up with incoming waste. In turn, the best way to rid the body of toxins is through the bowels. To be honest, I hoped to avoid the topic of colon health, especially for a recipe book! Nevertheless, for the sake of health and beauty, maintaining healthy bowels requires our attention.

Few people discuss elimination more than raw foodists. This is because raw food eaters experience superior digestion. They just can't keep quiet about it. Fresh fruits and vegetables provide abundant sources of fiber and living water, working together to cleanse, purify, and nourish the digestive tract. In contrast, constipation is a sore subject for some. A clogged and overburdened colon is no laughing matter. Constipation is a sign of health problems to come and acceleration in aging.

What is a healthy bowel movement anyway? Is it once per day as we're often told? For those on the Standard American Diet, eating three meals a day may produce one S.A.D. movement. No wonder it's normal for Americans to gain an average of a pound, or more, a year. On the other hand, raw foodists often experience eliminations equal to the number of meals they consume per day. Imagine being the same weight as you were in high school. The good news is for those suffering from constipation, increasing the amount of raw food in the diet can improve digestion, control weight gain, boost overall health, and enhance beauty.

Detoxification through Fasting

Is your digestive tract tired? Ever consider your organs needing a break?   The answer lies in fasting. The practice of abstaining from food—or both food and water—for a length of time is the process of fasting. Practiced for thousands of years for both spiritual and medicinal purposes, fasting is common in every region of the world.

From water fasts to juice fasts to whole food fasts, fasting promotes health and gives the body time to cleanse, rest, and heal. There are also elimination fasts, where certain foods are abstained from, such as particular types of meat or processed foods. There are even fasts where non-food related activities are given up to break unproductive habits, such as watching too much television.

Some consider those eating raw food already living a fasted lifestyle. In reality, many raw food eaters fast as part of their lifestyle. From seeking spiritual insight and mental clarity to promoting longevity and beauty, fasting is an investment with a significant return. As a rule, the longer the fast and less fiber consumed the deeper the cleanse. Some fast once per week while others fast an entire week or longer. If you are new to fasting, I recommend trying a fresh juice or green smoothie fast for one to five days and see how you feel.

Unfortunately, many fasters do more damage than good. How can this be? Sometimes good intentions reap unhealthy rewards. For starters, fasting is no quick-fix diet plan. Drinking empty-calories pumped with caffeinated stimulants, refined sweeteners, and chemical additives on an empty system is harmful and resembles more of an eating disorder than the life-giving benefits of fasting.

In addition, many break a fast only to experience indigestion and discomfort worse than before they even started. This happens because once the organs and digestive tract are clean, now accustomed to pure water, fresh juices, or raw foods, they often encounter surprise attacks by UFOs—unidentified *frankenfood* objects—due to their enlightened sensitivity to chemicals, antibiotics, and preservatives in foods. One may even discover an existing food allergy to a particular type of food just because the system is now clean enough to feel the difference. A good way to end a water or juice fast is to drink blended fruits and vegetables, such as the smoothies and soups in this book. Gradually work up to eating solid foods, keeping them as natural and organic as possible.

Detoxify Your Life and Live Light

Staying in motion is an important part of living light. I stretch and exercise at home as part of my morning routine. I used to be in competitive gymnastics, and although this was years ago I started lessons again to work on basic moves, improving strength and flexibility. Walking and dancing are two favorite activities as well. In short, whether playing basketball, golfing, gardening, or rock climbing, physical activity becomes habit-forming when it's enjoyed.

Another way to lighten the load is to detox one's environment by getting rid of unneeded clutter or giving away belongings no longer used. Coming home to a clean environment makes it easier to leave one's cares at the door. Lastly, resting is essential to health. In today's fast-paced world, many people feel they cannot afford to take one day off per week to rest. The pressures and expectations to work around the clock, however, can catch up with a person, leading to burn out and sickness. I find that taking a day to rest my mind, soul, and body not only increases my productivity level throughout the week, but it also improves my mood and overall outlook on life.

The Art of Dry Brushing

Dry brushing is a beauty secret few know about and even fewer practice. When I first heard about dry brushing, it seemed like a mysterious ritual practiced by health gurus to keep clean because they spent time in places without showers. However, after meeting my first dry brusher with fabulous skin, I decided to try it.

During the aging process, skin cell renewal slows down causing wrinkles to set in and skin to sag. To keep collagen and elastin plentiful, the best diet to consume is raw, living foods because they aid in the increase of cellular activity. While cell replication is the first step in maintaining youthful skin, exfoliation is the next step in keeping skin radiant. Dry brushing sloughs off dead skin cells, allowing porous skin to breathe and encouraging new skin cells to emerge.

This inexpensive practice of gently stroking the skin with a natural fiber brush or loofa gives the skin a silky, soft feeling. Dry brushing also breaks up cellulite directly under the skin's surface, especially those fat clumps around the hip and thigh area (this should be incentive enough to try dry brushing). In addition to firming and smoothing out the skin, a much deeper work is done as the lymphatic system is cleansed and the immune system is strengthened.

Choose a natural fiber brush, cloth, or loofa. Avoid using synthetic material on the skin. For hard-to-reach places, use a brush with a handle. Dry brushing strokes are light and gentle circular motions that feel soothing rather than scratchy. With each circular stroke, end upwards and in the direction of the heart. To get the glow, follow this five minute exercise daily.

- Start on the outside of the right foot, brush in circular motions moving up the leg. Then do the same on the inside of the leg. Repeat on the left leg.

- Brush large circular strokes on the right buttock. Repeat on the left side.

- Similar to the legs, brush the outside of the right hand moving up the arm. Then do the same on the inside of the arm. Repeat on the left arm.

- Brush the stomach in circular motions starting at the naval and work outward.

- Brush the lower back in circular motions moving outward and upward.

- Brush the right side of the ribcage moving upward. Repeat on the left side.

- Brush the breasts in circular motions, starting on the right side and avoiding the nipple area.

- Stroke the neck downward toward the heart.

- Avoiding the eye area, brush the face with outward and upward strokes.

Dry brushing the face is optional as many will think the face is too delicate. One option is to use a softer brush for the face than for the body. In fact, dry brushing the face increases circulation and tightens the skin. Due to increased cell renewal from eating raw foods, dry brushing my face is one way I maintain a clean, exfoliated surface. If suffering from acne or other skin disorders, avoid dry brushing those areas.

After dry brushing, rinse with warm water. The skin is now perfectly clean and there is no need to use abrasive soaps with harsh chemicals. Although dry brushing works as a natural cleanser, if you still like to use cleansers, use products with all natural ingredients. After rinsing, pat your skin with a towel. For more natural beauty secrets visit my tips at **www.dirtcheapbeautysecrets.com.**

List of ingredients for the following beauty recipes.

Essential Oils

Lavender Oil
Lemon Oil
Neroli Oil

Patchouli Oil
Peppermint Oil
Sweet Orange Oil

Other

Apple Cider Vinegar
Chlorella Powder
Hydrogen Peroxide (3 percent grade)

Spirulina Powder
Stevia Powder

Natural Minty Mouthwash

Used as a mouthwash or a toothpaste replacement, each ingredient has therapeutic or anti-bacterial properties, keeping bleeding and swelling gums down.

1 cup water
1 cup hydrogen peroxide
1/2 teaspoon stevia powder
1/4 teaspoon spirulina or chlorella

2 drops patchouli oil
2 drops sweet orange oil
1 drop peppermint oil

Blend or stir all ingredients together. Keep the amount you need in room temperature up to 2 weeks or in the refrigerator up to 2 months.
MAKES OVER 2 CUPS

Radiating Cucumber Mask

Whether eaten or applied externally, cucumbers are a classic beauty food for the skin.

Leftover pulp from the *Basil-Infused Cucumber Juice (see recipe page 22)*

1 tablespoon apple cider vinegar
1 tablespoon honey

Mix all ingredients together. Apply the mixture after making the *Basil-Infused Cucumber Juice* or store in the refrigerator up to 2 days. A chilled mask is extra refreshing and invigorates facial tissues. Leave the mask on for 10 minutes and rinse.

Nourishing Facial & Body Polish

This natural scrub exfoliates, keeping the skin silky smooth and balanced. The neroli and patchouli oils promote skin cell renewal, arresting premature aging.

1 cup leftover pulp from the *Almond Milk** (see recipe page 26)
1/2 cup honey

1/4 cup apple cider vinegar
2-5 drops neroli oil
2-5 drops patchouli oil

Mix all ingredients together. Gently massage the polish onto the body and face. Rinse with cool or warm water. Keep the amount you need in room temperature up to 3 days or in the refrigerator up to 2 weeks. **MAKES 1 3/4 CUPS**

*Other nut and seed pulp recipes in this book can be used in place of the almond pulp.

Skin Revitalizing Toner

Apply this toner after showering and before adding a base oil or facial cream. This toner awakens and balances the skin. Spray it on the face in the middle of the day as a refresher.

1 cup water
1/4 cup apple cider vinegar
2-3 drops lavender oil

2-3 drops neroli oil
2-3 drops patchouli oil

Mix all ingredients together and store in a glass jar or glass spray bottle. Dab or spray on the face and neck. Follow with a base oil or facial cream. Store the toner on the countertop up to 2 months. **MAKES 1 1/4 CUPS**

Nighttime Renewal Toner

Citrus oils help renew the skin during beauty sleep.

1 cup water
1/4 cup apple cider vinegar
1/4 cup hydrogen peroxide

3-5 drops lemon oil
3-5 drops sweet orange oil

Mix all ingredients together and store in a glass jar or glass spray bottle. Dab or spray on the face and neck. Follow with a base oil or facial cream. Store the toner on the countertop up to 2 months. **MAKES 1 1/2 CUPS**

INDEX

Dill Dressing, 54; in Asian Miso-Date Dressing, 57; in Spinach Pecan Salad with Blueberry-Date Dressing, 58; in Zucchini and Pumpkin Seed Hummus, 68; in Collard Green Dolmas, 86; in Lime Mousse with Mango Coulis, 93; in Frozen Chocolate Mousse Cake, 97; in Apple Pecan Crumble, 99; in Frosted Pumpkin Seed and Date Balls, 104

nut milks, how to make, 14, 16

nutritional yeast, 10, 12

Nuts for a Choco-Banana Smoothie, 32

Nutty Garlic Parmesan Topping, 56

O

Onion Sour Cream, recipe for, 64, 44, 48, 79, 80

onion: 9; in Creamy Broccoli Bisque, 42; in Summer Gazpacho, 48; in Zesty Cauliflower Pilaf, 62; in Onion Sour Cream, 64; in Stuffed Tomatoes, 79; in Collard Green Dolmas, 86

orange, 9, 20; in Citrus Cucumber Crush, 38; in I "C" Smoothie, 38; in Curried Mango Bisque, 40; in Chilled Mango and Coconut Cream Soup, 51; in Citrus and Sesame Dressing, 54; in Asian Miso-Date Dressing, 57; in Pecan Truffles, 102

organic, 7, 12, 13, 18, 108

P

parsley, 10, 20

pears, 9, 70

Pecan Truffles, 102, **103**

pecans: 10; in Spinach Pecan Salad with Blueberry-Date Dressing, 58, **59**; in Apple Pecan Crumble, 99; in Pecan Truffles, 102

Peppermint Cacao Energy Surge, 31

Peppermint Chocolate Mousse, 90, **91**

pepper, bell: 9; in Tomato Ginger Bisque, 44; in Yellow Bell Pepper Bisque with Basil, 46; in Summer Gazpacho, 48; in Peppery Spice Sunflower Ranch, 56; in Spicy Fusion Guacamole, 62; in Marinated Sesame and Mushroom Sushi Rolls, 74; in Tacos with Ground Walnut and Red Bell Pepper, 80; in Chinese Instant Noodles, 84

Peppery Spice Sunflower Ranch, 56

Pickled Sesame Cabbage, 60, **61**

Pistachio Peppermint Pudding, 94, **95**

pistachios, 10, 94

Pumpkin Seed and Sundried Tomato Pâté Wraps, 73

Pumpkin Seed Milk, recipe for, 26, 31, cream, 40; 93, 101

pumpkin seeds, 10; in Zucchini and Pumpkin Seed Hummus, 68; in Zucchini Fettuccini with Pumpkin Seed Pesto, 72; in Pumpkin Seed and Sundried Tomato Pâté Wraps, 73; in Spinach and Pumpkin Seed Manicotti, 77; in Frosted Pumpkin Seed and Date Balls, 104

R

Radiating Cucumber Mask, 113

raisins, 10; in Collard Green Dolmas, 86; in Super Green Cacao Energy Balls, 98; in Apple Pecan Crumble, 99; in Chocolate Layered Cherry Cream Tart, 101

Raspberry Greenade, 34

Ruby Red Blush, 24, **25**

S

seaweed, sea vegetables (nori), 10, 13; in Marinated Sesame and Mushroom Sushi Rolls, 74; in Almond & Sunflower Seed Pâté Sushi Rolls, 88

Sesame Seed Milk, 28

Skin Revitalizing Toner, 114

sodium chloride (table salt), 32, 88

Spicy Fusion Guacamole, 62

Spinach and Pumpkin Seed Manicotti, **76**, 77

Spinach Pecan Salad with Blueberry-Date Dressing, 58, **59**

Spinach, Mango, and Banana Smoothie, 31

spirulina, 10, 13

stevia, 14, 112, 113

Strawberry Calcium Boost, 36

Strawberry Tart with a Macadamia Nut Crust, 92

Stuffed Tomatoes, 79

Summer Gazpacho, 48, **49**

sunflower seeds, 10, 14; in Peppery Spice Sunflower Ranch, 56; in Zesty Cauliflower Pilaf, 62; in Tomato, Mushroom, and Spinach-Pesto Torte, 82; in Almond & Sunflower Seed Pâté Sushi Rolls, 88; in Super Green Cacao Energy Balls, 98

Super Green Cacao Energy Balls, 98

Sweet Almond and Red Date Cream, 30

Sweet and Spicy Red Pepper Mayo, 69

T

Tacos with Ground Walnut and Red Bell Pepper, 80, **81**

Tomato Ginger Bisque, 44, **45**

Tomato, Mushroom, and Spinach-Pesto Torte, 82, **83**

W

walnuts, 10; in Stuffed Tomatoes, 79; in Tacos with Ground Walnut and Red Bell
   Pepper, 80; in Frozen Chocolate Mousse Cake, 97; in Chocolate Layered
   Cherry Cream Tart, 101
Watermelon Juice with a Hint of Peppermint, 22
wheat grass powder, 10, 20

Y

Yellow Bell Pepper Bisque with Basil, 46

Z

Zesty Cauliflower Pilaf, 62, **63**
Zucchini and Pumpkin Seed Hummus, 68
Zucchini Fettuccini with Pumpkin Seed Pesto, 72

Made in the USA
San Bernardino, CA
11 January 2014